# Novell ZENworks 7 Linux Management

## Administrator's Handbook

RON TANNER
RICHARD WHITEHEAD

N
Novell
PRESS™
Novell.

Published by Pearson Education, Inc.
800 East 96th Street, Indianapolis, Indiana 46240 USA

# Novell ZENworks 7 Linux Management Administrator's Handbook

International Standard Book Number: 0-672-32784-8

Library of Congress Catalog Card Number: 2004195536

Printed in the United States of America

First Printing: September 2005

08  07  06  05        4   3   2   1

## Trademarks

## Warning and Disclaimer

## About Novell Press

Novell Press is the exclusive publisher of trade computer technology books that have been authorized by Novell, Inc. Novell Press books are written and reviewed by the world's leading authorities on Novell and related technologies, and are edited, produced, and distributed by the Que/Sams Publishing group of Pearson Education, the worldwide leader in integrated education and computer technology publishing. For more information on Novell Press and Novell Press books, please go to **www.novellpress.com**.

## Special and Bulk Sales

Pearson offers excellent discounts on this book when ordered in quantity for bulk purchases or special sales. For more information, please contact

U.S. Corporate and Government Sales
1-800-382-3419
corpsales@pearsontechgroup.com

For sales outside of the U.S., please contact

International Sales
international@pearsoned.com

**ASSOCIATE PUBLISHER**
Mark Taber

**PROGRAM MANAGER**
Novell, Inc.
Darrin Vandenbos

**MARKETING MANAGER**
Doug Ingersoll

**ACQUISITIONS EDITOR**
Jenny Watson

**DEVELOPMENT EDITOR**
Scott Meyers

**MANAGING EDITOR**
Charlotte Clapp

**PROJECT EDITOR**
George Nedeff

**COPY EDITOR**
Margo Catts

**INDEXER**
Ken Johnson

**PROOFREADER**
Jessica McCarty

**TECHNICAL EDITOR**
Jason Blackett

**PUBLISHING COORDINATOR**
Vanessa Evans

**BOOK DESIGNER**
Gary Adair

**PAGE LAYOUT**
Toi Davis

# Contents at a Glance

# Table of Contents

**CHAPTER 8:  Catalogs**    **99**

**CHAPTER 9:  Policies**    **107**

# Preface

The Open Source Software movement continues to shape the dynamics of the computer software industry as it has for the last decade. At the center of the Open Source Software is Linux—an operating system whose rapid growth is changing the world's perception of open source.

Strong backing by companies, such as Novell, who provide Linux distributions (SUSE LINUX, Novell Linux Desktop) along with all the necessary services and support functions, help make Linux an acceptable operating system choice for businesses. As a consequence, corporations are beginning to make significant movements to incorporate Linux into their business-critical computing systems. With the advent of the Novell Linux Desktop and other desktop offerings, Linux will also grow in the end-user desktop environment.

As the Linux operating system becomes more prevalent in back-end server and desktop systems, companies will need better management systems to reduce the cost of Linux ownership. Companies cannot tolerate the high level of manual and complex tasks that are required to manage Linux systems. It is inefficient and costly to spend resources on doing mundane tasks such as hauling mounds of CDs around to install applications on users' computers, re-installing operating systems, searching for all those dependent RPMs, or trying to figure out where the Linux assets are.

ZENworks provides a management solution with a proven record of reducing the total cost of ownership. ZENworks helps you manage your systems through their entire life cycle. With ZENworks, the system automatically tracks assets; delivers applications; keeps your laptops, workstations, and servers up to date on the latest approved patches; and finds all of those dependent RPMs. ZENworks even delivers images to those systems that need restoring or upgrading. ZENworks includes remote management capabilities to help you diagnose and control computers in your WAN or across the Internet.

ZENworks delivers all these features into your enterprise regardless of your preferred platform. ZENworks can function in a Windows-only environment or mixed environments, including Windows, NetWare, and Linux.

This book is about installing and getting ZENworks Linux Management working in your environment, from small to enterprise levels. We try to point out all the tips and "gotchas" to watch for to make your installation and deployment of ZENworks Linux Management a success.

We thank you for purchasing this book and hope that it is useful to you.

# About the Authors

**Ron Tanner** is currently a product manager for Novell ZENworks, defining the future of the product. Ron has been associated with ZENworks since its inception, and lead software development as Director of Engineering through the invention and first releases of ZENworks. He has 20 years of experience in developing software and leading engineering teams into exciting, cutting-edge technology. Prior to working at Novell, Ron developed advanced networking systems at AT&T Bell Laboratories. Ron has co-authored six other ZENworks Novell Press titles. When Ron can sneak away from ZENworks he can be found having fun with his wife, CheRee, and his four children, Teagan, Matson, Kellyn, and Jarett.

**Richard Whitehead** is currently the Director of Product Marketing for Novell ZENworks. Richard has worked on ZENworks for many years in various roles, including Product Line Manager. He has over 15 years of experience in the software industry, holding senior positions as a software engineer, tester, evangelist, product manager, and product marketing manager. In addition to working for Novell, Richard has worked for Evans and Sutherland, WordPerfect, and Citrix. In his free time, Richard enjoys just being a homebody, working in the yard, playing sports, and spending as much time as possible with his wife, Sandy, and three children Mitchell, Christian, and Madison.

# Dedication

*To the family, thanks for encouraging my writing. To my sweetheart and soulmate, thanks for the last 25 years. I'm looking forward to the next 25. And to my Novell buddies, thanks for being the best to work with, and working so hard to make something great. The future can be even better.*

—Ron Tanner

*To my wonderful family whose zeal for life keeps me going. To my forever friend and companion, you are my one and only. To Twixinator, Dottinator, Schmooklinator, Cheese, and Snitch. To all those I work with that make my job so great. Your dedication, talent, and friendship will continue to make Novell a great place to work. Thanks for building the best product in the market.*

—Richard Whitehead

# Acknowledgments

Our sincere gratitude goes out to the following persons, without whom this book could not have happened:

To the ZENworks team that keeps working hard to make a great product even better. We're looking forward to the next version. We know it will propel ZENworks to new areas.

To everyone at Novell who allowed us to pick their brains, including but not limited to (with apologies to any whose names we have forgotten): Ty Ellis, Ken Muir, Jose Mercado, Dan Montroy, Abhay Padlia, Brian Vaughan, Jason Brothers, Jawaad Tariq, Mauro Miranda, Steve Faber, and Mark Roberts.

To our editors who make the book readable, check us on our technical accuracy, and kept us on track, you all are great (and picky). It seems that nothing gets by you. Thanks to Matthew Purcell, Jenny Watson, George Nedeff, and Margo Catts. And special thanks to Jason Blackett who kept us honest.

# We Want to Hear from You!

As the reader of this book, *you* are our most important critic and commentator. We value your opinion and want to know what we're doing right, what we could do better, what topics you'd like to see us cover, and any other words of wisdom you're willing to pass our way.

You can email or write me directly to let me know what you did or didn't like about this book—as well as what we can do to make our books better.

*Please note that I cannot help you with technical problems related to the topic of this book and that due to the high volume of mail I receive I may not be able to reply to every message.*

When you write, please be sure to include this book's title and author as well as your name and email address or phone number. I will carefully review your comments and share them with the author and editors who worked on the book.

Email:  feedback@novellpress.com

Mail:  Mark Taber
Associate Publisher
Novell Press/Pearson Education
800 East 96th Street
Indianapolis, IN 46240 USA

# Reader Services

For more information about this book or others from Novell Press, visit our website at www.novellpress.com. Type the ISBN or the title of a book in the Search field to find the page you're looking for.

# CHAPTER 1

# The Evolution of Linux Management

In August 2003, Novell acquired a company called Ximian. Ximian was founded with the goal of building enterprise-class Linux solutions. One of these solutions was called Red Carpet, which was initially built to help Ximian Desktop customers keep their Linux systems up to date. Because a Linux system is basically a collection of packages (RPMs), the Ximian engineers built Red Carpet to deal with the multiple RPM dependencies. Red Carpet consisted of two components. The first component was the Red Carpet Daemon, an open source daemon which could be used to get software updates for one system at a time. The second component was called Red Carpet Enterprise, which was a proprietary, inside-the-firewall solution that enabled enterprises to manage their Linux systems centrally. Shortly after acquiring Ximian, Novell re-branded Red Carpet Enterprise to ZENworks Linux Management.

This book discusses the features and capabilities of ZENworks 7 Linux Management. ZENworks 7 Linux Management is a major release to ZENworks Linux Management, and it includes many new capabilities that aren't found in other Linux management products. ZENworks 7 Linux Management brings to the Linux platform many of the features that current ZENworks customers have been using on Windows. However, ZENworks 7 Linux Management is built on a brand-new service-oriented architecture (SOA). This new architecture will be adopted by other ZENworks products in future releases.

# What's the Big Deal?

Linux is maturing rapidly and is being deployed by more and more enterprises. Just like Windows, an enterprise operating system must be manageable. Without good resource management, it is nearly impossible to provide a secure and stable IT environment. ZENworks 7 Linux Management enables administrators to use state-of-the-art tools for deployment, management, and ongoing maintenance of all their Linux systems.

# The ZENworks Family

Because many readers of this book will be existing ZENworks customers, it's important to understand the entire ZENworks family and the role that ZENworks Linux Management plays. Although ZENworks Linux Management is available separately, it is also available as part of the ZENworks Suite—an integrated resource management solution for deploying, managing, and maintaining desktops, servers, and handheld devices throughout their lifecycle across multiple platforms. The capabilities in the ZENworks Suite include the following:

- **ZENworks Desktop Management**—Automates the configuration, deployment, updating, healing, and migration of desktops. ZENworks Desktop Management also includes ZENworks Patch Management, ZENworks Data Management, ZENworks Personality Migration, and ZENworks Software Packaging.

- **ZENworks Server Management**—Automates server configuration and the distribution and inventory of applications, content, and patches across all servers, regardless of platform. ZENworks Server Management also includes ZENworks Software Packaging and ZENworks Patch Management.

- **ZENworks Handheld Management**—Automates handheld device management to reduce high ownership costs, strengthen security, and increase user productivity on Palm, Windows CE, Pocket PC, and RIM BlackBerry devices.

- **ZENworks Data Management**—Automatically backs up and synchronizes user files and data across multiple devices and even the Internet to reduce the costs of lost data, data restoration, and data access help desk calls.

- **ZENworks Personality Migration**—Automates the migration of personal settings and application settings for each desktop for OS migration or disaster recovery.

- **ZENworks Software Packaging**—Automates the repackaging, customizing, and distribution of MSI applications.

- **ZENworks Patch Management**—Automates detection, deployment, and defending of Windows patches.

- **ZENworks Linux Management**—Uses policies to automate the deployment, management, and maintenance of Linux resources. These automated and intelligent policies provide centralized control across the lifecycle of Linux systems with desktop lockdown, imaging, remote management, inventory, and software management.

All ZENworks products rely significantly on the directory, specifically Novell eDirectory, to provide a greater level of manageability, and greater ease of management, for each component in the network.

Most ZENworks products are cross platform and can run not only in NetWare environments, but also in Windows and Linux environments (without the need for NetWare or the Novell Windows client).

# What's New for ZENworks 7 Linux Management?

There are many new features and capabilities in ZENworks 7 Linux Management. In addition to a new architecture, new features include the following:

- ZENworks Control Center, for web-based administration

- New reporting capabilities

- Imaging of Linux servers and desktops

- Remote control

- Policy-based management

- Hardware and software inventory

# Using ZENworks Linux Management with Novell Linux Desktop

ZENworks Linux Management is not only complementary to Novell Linux Desktop, it is critical. ZENworks Linux Management enables you to deploy, manage, and maintain your Novell Linux Desktops centrally and includes the capability to image a desktop, deliver and install software, keep the desktop up to date, and control the desktop remotely for help desk and troubleshooting.

ZENworks Linux Management also provides lockdown policies specific to Novell Linux Desktop that make it possible to apply policies to devices to configure and potentially protect and lock down the device from user modifications. This enables you to configure your Linux systems as you need them to be to work most effectively in your personalized environments. Then you can rest assured that the users of these devices will not be able to disrupt their Linux systems by reconfiguring your locked policies.

ZENworks Linux Management introduces the following policies to the Linux environment: Epiphany Policy, Evolution Policy, GNOME Policy, Novell Linux Desktop Policy, Remote Execute Policy, and Text File Policy. With these policies you can manage your Linux systems and the applications that run on them.

With the Novell Linux Desktop Policy you can configure whether screen locking is on, determine background images for your desktops and the themes you want for your corporation, and enable and disable applets, including Dictionary, Sticky Notes, OpenOffice Quickstart, and so on. These and other settings enable you to configure your systems exactly as you want them for your users.

Additionally, with the Novell Linux Desktop Policy you control whether the configurations you place down on the initial desktops are locked from user changes, or which configurations you will allow your users to customize.

**NOTE**

The ZENworks Linux Management Agent is installed by default with Novell Linux Desktop. This makes it easy to register and manage Novell Linux Desktop out of the box.

# Using ZENworks Linux Management with SUSE LINUX Enterprise Server

ZENworks Linux Management is also available as a bundle with SUSE LINUX Enterprise Server 9. Together they provide the most powerful, secure, and manageable Linux solution in the market by giving IT administrators centralized control over Linux software configurations across their server and workstation infrastructures. Although ZENworks Linux Management is tightly integrated with SUSE LINUX Enterprise Server 9 (which is also part of Novell Open Enterprise Server), it also supports and manages Red Hat.

Novell ZENworks Linux Management enables administrators to easily configure, update, secure, and manage SUSE LINUX Enterprise Server 9 from a central location, providing enterprise-level IT management across the entire organization.

Just like Novell Linux Desktop, the ZENworks Linux Management Agent is installed by default with SUSE LINUX Enterprise Server.

# CHAPTER 2

# Understanding ZENworks Linux Management

## General Architecture

ZENworks Linux Management is built on an all-new Services Oriented Architecture (SOA). This architecture represents significant advancements for existing ZENworks customers and is probably a familiar architecture for current ZENworks Linux Management users. Service Oriented Architectures are more scalable, Internet friendly, and secure. This section discusses the ZENworks Linux Management architecture, components, and best practices for rollout.

The first server that you install is called the *primary* ZENworks server. Additional ZENworks servers, called *secondary* servers, can be set up and then "joined" to the primary server. The only difference between the primary ZENworks server and the other secondary ZENworks servers is that the database is installed on the primary server. A collection of ZENworks servers is called a *zone*. ZENworks zones should be on a single LAN for better performance and scalability.

Two main components are typically installed on the primary ZENworks server:

- The database that contains the RPM packages to be delivered, device information, hardware and software inventory, and scheduled actions.

- The ZENworks Object Store, where the device objects, content objects, group memberships, and object relationships are stored.

Every Managed Device, including the ZENworks server(s), has the ZENworks Management Agent. This agent uses the Mono (.NET) runtime environment on which the web services for policies, packages, remote control, and inventory run. In addition to the ZENworks Management Agent, the ZENworks Server has the following components (see Figure 2.1):

- Java runtime for Tomcat to run the ZENworks Control Center

- Java runtime for Tiered Electronic Distribution

- PDHCP server for proxy DHCP

- Imaging server

- TFTP server

**FIGURE 2.1**
ZENworks Linux Management architecture.

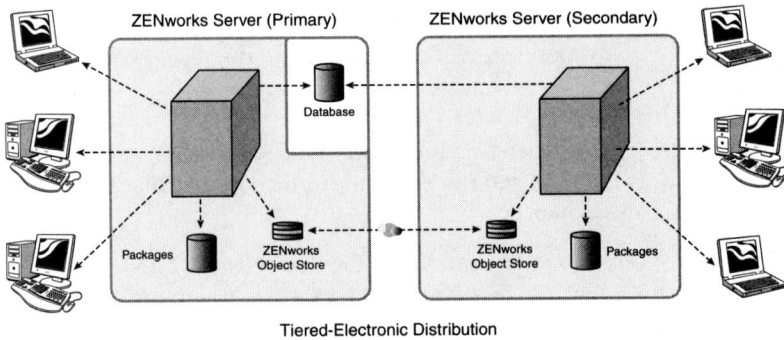

# Open Source Components

ZENworks Linux Management can be divided into two components: the ZENworks Server and the ZENworks Management Agent. The ZENworks Server is the center point of ZENworks Linux Management and runs the services for the system. The ZENworks Server is proprietary and not open source. The ZENworks Management Agent, on the other hand, is open source and enables Linux systems to be managed by the ZENworks Server.

If there isn't a ZENworks Linux Management server within your environment, users can receive "updates" from public servers only. This is a good solution for individual users, but is not recommended for enterprises.

# Best Practices of Rollout Procedures

It is highly recommended that you create a primary ZENworks server within the same LAN of the managed devices, meaning that you do not manage devices over a WAN. This is also true for additional ZENworks servers that you "join" to the primary. The additional servers that are joined will point back to the primary server for the database, the ZENworks Object Stores are replicated, and the packages are distributed via Tiered-Electronic Distribution. It will be faster and more efficient to have these processes done within a high-speed LAN environment.

# Use of Directories

As with other ZENworks products, ZENworks Linux Management uses Novell eDirectory to provide secure, scalable, policy-driven management. This is referred to as the *ZENworks Object Store* and is actually Novell eDirectory 8.7.3, which is automatically installed and configured during the setup of the ZENworks server. This means that behind the scenes you are using the strengths of eDirectory for replication, federation, and object management. For the most part, you do not need to worry about maintenance on the ZENworks Object Store. However, if needed, you can use the standard eDirectory tools.

# Use of Existing Databases

Out of the box, ZENworks Linux Management ships with the Postgres database. If you choose to use Postgres, ZENworks Linux Management auto-matically sets it up and installs it. This includes applying the schema.

In many enterprises, you may already have Oracle running and have trained Oracle database administrators. ZENworks Linux Management can also use Oracle 9i. You must have Oracle 9i running on a different server than the ZENworks server. Also, you need to take some other steps to configure Oracle 9i with ZENworks Linux Management.

Before installing the ZENworks server, first ensure that you have connectivity between the server on which you will be installing and the Oracle server. You also need to apply the ZENworks schema. Then, during the install of the ZENworks server, you will be prompted on the database you want to use. Choose Oracle 9i and enter the DNS or IP address of the database server. You can get more information about database setup in Chapter 3, "Installing ZENworks Linux Management."

## Use of Existing Servers

Because the ZENworks server uses HTTP/HTTPS (ports 80 and 443), it is best practice to have a dedicated server. Otherwise, other web services that also use ports 80/443 could conflict with ZENworks Linux Management services. Using a dedicated server also provides additional disk space that may be required for RPM packages and the other items stored in the Postgres database.

## How and Where ZENworks Linux Management Is Managed

The ZENworks server is also considered to be a managed device. This means that you can manage and maintain the ZENworks server(s) just like any other managed device.

ZENworks Linux Management uses a web-based interface called the ZENworks Control Center. Using the ZENworks Control Center you can manage all your Linux systems from a central location. We recommend that you take some time to familiarize yourself with the ZENworks Control Center, especially if you are an existing ZENworks customer.

## How Devices Are Represented and Managed in ZLM

Every managed device is displayed in the ZENworks Control Center. The process for bringing a device into the Control Center is called *registration*. During the registration process, you can determine the containment of the device through a registration key. You can read more about registration keys in Chapter 5, "Registering Devices into the System."

After a device is accessible within the ZENworks Control Center, you can perform inventory, deliver and install software, enforce policies, and remote control the device. All these capabilities are done through the ZENworks Management Agent.

# How Content Is Delivered

Because ZENworks Linux Management uses a web services model, all work is done on the server and not the client or managed device. Requests are made by the ZENworks Management Agent, using a web service. The server then processes the request and provides a response back to the agent. This results in a system that is not "chatty" and using up bandwidth within the network. This process is illustrated in Figure 2.2.

**FIGURE 2.2**
ZENworks system overview.

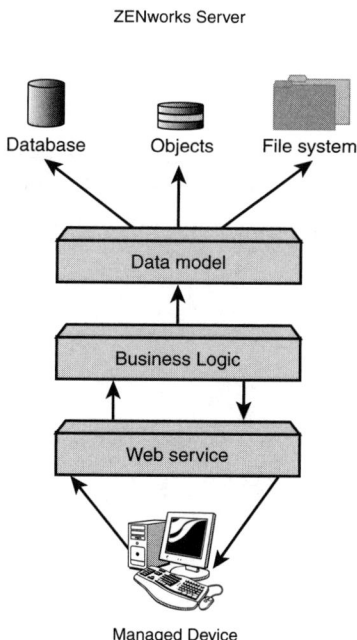

ZENworks Server

Database          Objects          File system

Data model

Business Logic

Web service

Managed Device

# Terminology/Glossary

**ZENworks Primary Server**—This is the first server installed. It contains the database, object store, and other web services.

**ZENworks Secondary Server**—These are any servers that are installed and "joined" to the primary server. It includes all the services that the primary server has except for the database.

**ZONE**—This is the management domain that includes the primary server and all secondary servers within a LAN.

**ZENworks Management Agent**—This is the agent that allows ZENworks Linux Management to manage the device.

**Registration Key**—The key used to register the device with the ZENworks server.

**ZENworks Control Center**—The web-based administration console used to administer ZENworks Linux Management.

**Managed Device**—Any device (workstation or server) that is managed by ZENworks Linux Management.

**Packages**—Installation files used to install software. These are also called *RPM packages*.

**Bundles**—A collection of packages.

**Postgres**—An open source database that can be used to store packages, inventory, and other device information for ZENworks Linux Management.

**ZENworks Object Store**—Stores the objects for the devices, content, and the object relationships.

# CHAPTER 3

# Installing ZENworks Linux Management

This chapter provides a walk-through on getting all the components of ZENworks Linux Management working in your environment. You always need to install a ZENworks primary server first, and then you can install agent components and secondary servers in any order you desire.

## Preparing the Server

In this step, you set up and prepare a server to host the ZLM server components. This server has similar requirements to a web or database server, and must be set up according to the following guidelines:

- A dedicated server running SUSE LINUX Enterprise Server 9 SP1 (SLES 9 SP1). It is recommended that you perform a new installation of SLES 9 with at least the default graphical base system. This system must not have any previous version of ZENworks Linux Management or Red Carpet installed.

- This server must be able to resolve client hostnames using some method (DNS, /etc/hosts/, and so on). A fully qualified domain name entry for each managed device in /etc/hosts should be sufficient for a test environment.

- A static IP address must be used when configuring the network on this server. You might encounter problems with the datastore configuration if the IP address is obtained from a DHCP server.

- No service should be running on port 80. If Apache is running on your server (or any other service binding to port 80), stop this service before installing ZENworks. Apache can be stopped with the following command: `/etc/init.d/apache2 stop`.

After you have completed this server configuration, you are ready to install ZENworks Linux Management.

# Executing the Installation Script

ZENworks Linux Management is composed of primary and secondary servers. The following sections describe how to install each of these types of servers.

## Installing a Primary Server

Run the following steps to install a ZENworks Linux Management primary server:

1. Insert the ZENworks Linux Management CD.

2. Log in as root and mount the installation media.

3. Change to the `/media/cdrom` (or device mounted in step 2) directory, where the CD was mounted.

4. Run the installation script: `./zlm-install`.

5. First the installation program verifies and installs Python, if necessary. Then you are prompted as to whether you wish to install ZENworks on this machine. Respond with a **y**.

6. You next are presented with the ZENworks License Agreement. Review the agreement, and then you are prompted to answer whether you accept the license agreement. Enter a **y** to accept.

7. The installation next installs the daemon that installs packages onto the system. The installation then begins installing dependent packages on the server. The installation creates a log file in the `/var/opt/novell/log/zenworks` directory.

8. After the dependencies are installed, the script installs the ZENworks software and data store components. Following these, it installs the administration tools and the preboot imaging services.

9. Next the installation script installs mirroring software to keep your ZENworks back-end servers synchronized, followed by the web services loader daemon and the ZENworks agent for the server.

10. Now that all the packages have been installed, the server needs to be configured. You are prompted to decide whether you wish to run zlm-config. Respond with a **y**.

11. The system gathers information and then prompts you for answers to the following:

    - Answer a **y** when asked whether this is the first server in the zone.

    - When prompted for an Organizational Name enter a unique name for this Management Zone.

    - When prompted, enter an Administrator password for accessing the web-based ZENworks Control Center, or the zlman command-line interface.

12. Next the installation asks whether you want to use an external database for your data store. If you choose to use the local database from ZENworks, then enter an **n** and continue. If you choose a **y** to store data in a database on another machine, enter the following, when prompted:

    - IP Address or host name of the database server.

    - Communication port to the database.

    - Database name.

    - Database user. This user must have write access to the database to create tables and then fill those tables with data.

    - Database user password.

13. ZENworks then completes the configuration of the remainder of the components.

## Installing a Secondary Server

A secondary server must be synchronized with the same clock time as the primary server. Be sure to complete the processes necessary to ensure time synchronization before installing the secondary server software.

You can run the following to configure NTP to an external timing source and to verify that you are synchronizing properly before your installation:

1. Determine the IP address of the server that is providing the clock. The primary and secondary can point to the same source, or you could have secondary servers point to the primary.

2. Launch YAST and select Network Services and NTP Client under that.

3. On the NTP Client Configuration screen, select to automatically start the daemon when booting the system.

4. In the NTP Server field enter the IP address of the server that will be providing the clock.

5. Select Finish to save the configuration and launch the daemon.

To verify that the timing synchronization is functioning properly, enter the ntpq -p command and verify that the offset field is less than 1 second.

Run the following steps to install a ZENworks Linux Management Secondary server:

1. Insert the ZENworks Linux Management CD.

2. Log in as root and mount the installation media.

3. Change to the /media/cdrom directory, where the CD was mounted.

4. Run the installation script ./zlm-install.

5. First the installation program verifies and installs Python, if necessary. Then you are prompted as to whether you wish to install ZENworks on this machine. Respond with a y.

6. Next you are presented with the ZENworks License Agreement. Review the agreement and then enter a y to accept.

7. The installation next installs the daemon that installs packages onto the system. The installation then begins installing dependent packages on the server. The installation creates a log file in the /var/opt/novell/log/zenworks directory.

8. After the dependencies are installed, the script installs the ZENworks software and data store components. It then installs the administration tools and the preboot imaging services.

9. Next the installation script installs mirroring software to keep your ZENworks back-end servers synchronized, followed by the web services loader daemon and the ZENworks agent for the server.

10. Now that all the packages have been installed, the server needs to be configured. You are prompted whether you wish to run zlm-config. Respond with a y.

11. The system gathers information and then prompts you for the following:

- Answer with an **n** when asked whether this is the first server in the zone.

- When prompted for an IP Address or DNS Name of Primary Server, enter the DNS name of the primary server in the zone. This server will then be a secondary server in that same zone.

- When prompted, enter the Administrator password for administrating the zone. This is the same password entered for the administrator when the primary server was installed.

   **12.** ZENworks then finishes configuring the remainder of the components.

After the installation process completes, verify the installation by following the instructions in the next section.

# Verifying the Installation

When the installation is complete, the ZENworks Management Daemon (zmd) is running on your server. Confirm this using the following command:

`/etc/init.d/novell-zmd status`

This status should be reported as running.

Confirm that the additional ZENworks services are running by using the following commands:

```
/etc/init.d/novell-zenloader status
/etc/init.d/novell-zenserver status
/etc/init.d/postgresql status
/etc/init.d/ndsd status
/etc/init.d/novell-zented status
/etc/init.d/novell-zmgprebootpolicy status
/etc/init.d/novell-pbserv status
/etc/init.d/novell-proxydhcp status
/etc/init.d/novell-zislnx status
/etc/init.d/novell-tftp status
```

Each of these services should be listed as running. If any services are not running, start them manually with the following command:

`/etc/init.d/<servicename> start`

After you have verified that these services are all running, you can log in to the ZENworks Control Center.

# Accessing the ZENworks Control Center

The ZENworks Control Center is a comprehensive web management interface to your ZENworks Linux Management environment. During installation, the ZENworks Control Center is installed, configured, and started on port 80 of your server.

The ZENworks Control Center supports the Firefox and Internet Explorer 6 SP1 browsers.

Additionally, you must have the Java 1.4 web browser plug-ins to use the Remote Management feature in the ZENworks Control Center. Visit Java.com (http://www.java.com) to obtain the 1.4 plug-in.

Access the ZENworks Control Center by opening a supported web browser to the following URL:

https://*zlmserver*

Replace *zlmserver* with the actual DNS name or IP address of your ZENworks server.

**NOTE**

The ZENworks Control Center requires an https:// connection; requests to http:// are redirected to https://.

When prompted for login credentials, use the Administrator user with the password you provided during the installation.

# Installing the Client Software on Managed Devices

Each client must meet the following requirements:

1. One of the following supported platforms:
   - SLES9 SP1 x86, Opteron, EM64T
   - Novell Linux Desktop SP1 x86, Opteron, EM64T
   - SUSE 9.3 x86, Opteron, EM64T
   - RHEL3 AS/ES/WS x86
   - RHEL4 AS/ES/WS x86

2. For Firefox policies to be available, the GConf-enabled version of Firefox provided with ZENworks Linux management release must be installed.

3. For NLD policies to be available, the NLD lockdown RPMs provided with the ZENworks release must be installed.

The client software installation uses the same installation source files and script as the server, although it is executed with a flag (-a) to indicate it is an agent-only installation.

Execute the following to install the client software:

1. Log in as root on the managed device.

2. From the directory you extracted the installation archive, run the following command to start the installation script:

   ```
   ./zlm-install -a
   ```

3. During installation, you are asked to provide the DNS name or IP address of the ZENworks server that will manage this device.

4. Optionally, you can provide a registration key, which determines the naming scheme and assignments this device receives.

If no registration key is provided, the default registration rules are applied.

You can also register this device manually any time after the installation completes by using the command-line tool **rug** that is installed on the device. The command **rug sl** lists the services with which you have registered. The command **rug sd #** removes the service specified. The command **rug sa** URL registers the device to the specified service.

After the installation has completed, the ZENworks Management Daemon (zmd) is running on this client. Confirm this using the following command:

```
/etc/init.d/novell-zmd status
```

This status should be listed as running.

If you used the default registration, you can also verify that this device is listed in the ZENworks Control Center.

# Upgrading ZENworks Linux Management from Previous Versions

ZENworks 7 Linux Management has a very different architecture than previous releases. For example, ZENworks 7 Linux Management has introduced an object store to manage the system. Consequently there is a migration process involved in moving to this version.

You can use two techniques to move information from your existing ZENworks Linux Management system to the new ZENworks 7 Linux Management installation: synchronization or migration.

The synchronization method copies the RPM files and brings them into the new system, whereas the migration method imports the database along with the RPM files. Both methods require that the new agent be installed on the device for it to be managed by the new system.

Because of the information length of time to migrate the database, and because the migration brings over only the package information, it is preferable to use the synchronization method to bring your packages over from your ZENworks Linux Management 6.6 system. After that synchronization is complete, redirect your new ZENworks 7 to the Novell corporate update site.

## Synchronization Method

The synchronization method requires that you retrieve channels from your existing ZENworks Linux Management 6.6 installation just as you would synchronizing other Linux sources into ZENworks 7 Linux Management. See Chapter 12, "Keeping ZENworks Linux Management Servers Synchronized," for more detailed information.

Channels in the existing system will become bundles in the new system. They are placed in a catalog that is assigned to all the devices, allowing them to retrieve all the updated RPMs.

When the agent is installed on the device, the device registers with the new ZENworks 7 system and then begins receiving its updates from there. To install the agent you can place the ZENworks 7 agent RPMs into a channel and then have the device perform a transaction to run the setup. Be sure to modify the configuration files to point your devices to the new ZENworks 7 system.

The synchronization method gets all the RPMs and channels over to your new system. The inventory is regenerated by the new system. Transactions are not available in the new system and have to be re-created with a Remote Execute policy.

## Migration Method

The migration method delivers all the database information that is relevant along with the files for the RPMs. This step, however, requires some manual administration.

Complete the following steps to migrate your system to the new ZENworks 7:

1. Log in to the existing ZENworks 6.6.x system as root.

2. Dump the existing ZENworks database by executing the following command:

   ```
   pg_dump -R -c -f rcserver.dump rcserver -U rcadmin
   ```

   This creates a dump of the database.

3. Copy the resulting dumped database and all the packages from the /ximian directory over to the new ZENworks 7 system using the secure copy command:

   ```
   scp -r rcserver.dump /ximian root@<server>
   ```

   This copies the files to the home directory of root on the target server.

4. The next step is to create a new database on the new ZENworks 7 Linux Management server and load the dumped information into this new database. Log in to the ZENworks 7 server as root and execute the following::

   a. Verify zlm-upgrade is in your path. It should be located at /opt/novell/zenworks/bin/zlm-upgrade.

   b. Retrieve the password to the ZENworks database by doing a cat /etc/opt/novell/zenworks/secretserver and capturing the output.

   c. Switch to postgres user with the su - postgres command.

   d. Create the database you need by entering the following command:

   ```
   postgres@server:/# createdb -U zenadmin zlm661
   ```

   When prompted for the password, enter the output from the secretserver file.

   e. Type Ctrl+D to return to root user.

   f. Now that the database is created, you need to configure postgres to use it. Do this by editing the /var/lib/pqsql/data/pq_hba.conf file and add the following entries:

   | local | zlm661 | zenadmin | md5 |
   |-------|--------|----------|-----|
   | host  | zlm661 | zenadmin | 0.0.0.0.0.0.0.0 md5 |

   Save the file.

g. Enter the command **/etc/init.d/postgresql restart** and wait for the database to finish coming up.

h. Enter the following to import the dumped data into the zlm661 database:

```
psql -U zenadmin zlm661 <rcserver.dump
```

When prompted for a password, enter the key from the secretserver file.

5. Run the following command to migrate the data from the database and the file system packages into ZENworks 7:

```
/opt/novell/zenworks/bin/zlm-upgrade zlm661 zenadmin ximian/red-
carpet-server <password from secretserver file>
```

6. When these steps are completed, the temporary database may be removed. Now all the package information, channels, and so on have been brought into ZENworks 7. Additionally, the administrators have been created in the new system and the RPM files have been copied into the proper locations.

# CHAPTER 4

# Understanding the ZENworks Control Center

This chapter discusses the main administration console for ZENworks 7 Linux Management, the ZENworks Control Center (ZCC).

## What Is the ZENworks Control Center?

The ZENworks Control Center is the heart of ZENworks 7 Linux Management. It is a task-oriented, web-based management console. If you prefer text-based administration, you can use ZLMAN. You can learn more about ZLMAN commands in Appendix A, "Commands."

The ZENworks Control Center is divided into three primary regions (see Figure 4.1). These regions are the Banner, the Navigation Bar, and the Content region. The Content region is further divided into the Header and the View.

**FIGURE 4.1**
Views within the ZENworks Control Center.

Banner

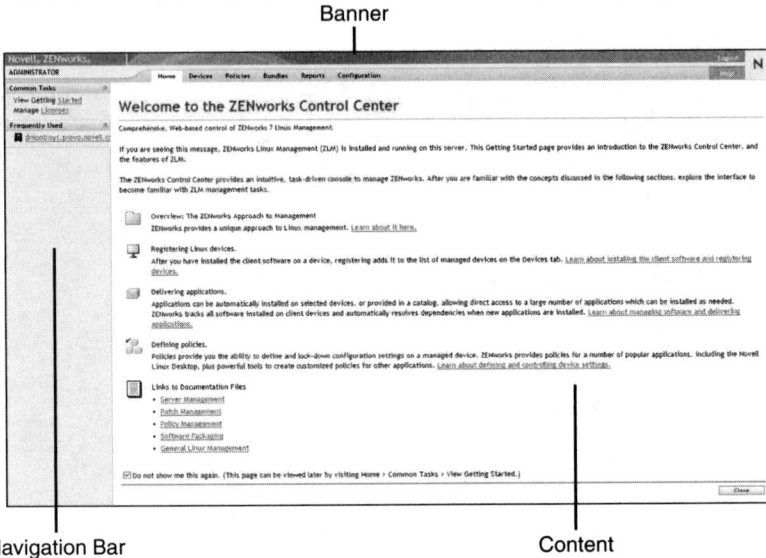

Navigation Bar                                                    Content

# The Banner

The Banner at the top of the ZENworks Control Center is always displayed. The contents of the Banner do not change. Within the Banner you find the Novell branding along with two other options. Clicking on Logout logs you out of the ZENworks Control Center and returns you to the login screen. Clicking on Help takes you to the help options, where you can get detailed help about the ZENworks Control Center.

The Banner also contains tabs for easier navigation of tasks. From left to right, these tabs are Home, Devices, Policies, Bundles, Reports, Configurations. Clicking on the Home tab takes you back to your default startup page, or to the last task you were doing on that page. Details about the other tabs can be found in their corresponding chapters.

Clicking on the Novell N on the far right of the Banner takes you to www.novell.com.

## Content Views

The Content region is the main area where tasks are performed. There are four different Content Views: the Portal View, the List View, the Settings View, and the Wizard View.

### PORTAL VIEW

The Portal View is one of the views you will see most often in the ZENworks Control Center. A Portal View is made up of several self-contained subcomponents called *snapshots*. Each snapshot contains information about a specific part of the system being managed. In Figure 4.2, you can see an example of a workstation Portal View that contains a snapshot for the hardware summary, as well as a snapshot for the effective policies. There is no limit to the number of snapshots that can be displayed in a Portal View.

**FIGURE 4.2**
Workstation Portal View.

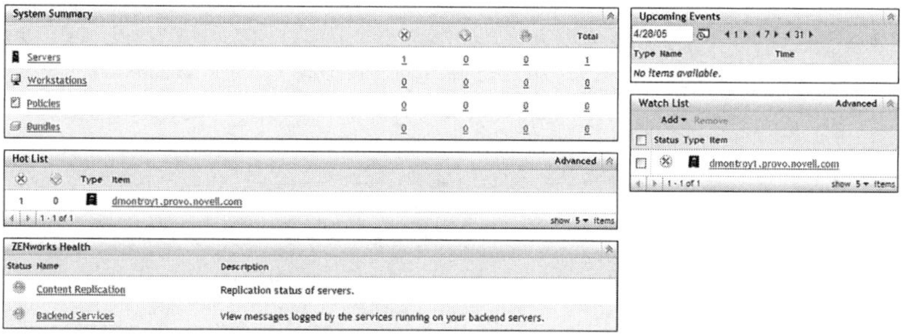

# List View

The List View, as you can envision from the name, shows a list of information from data sources like the database and the ZENworks Object Store. The information in the List Views enables you to easily sort, search, and perform actions on the data. Figure 4.3 shows an example of a server list view. In this view you can sort on any column, add or remove columns, as well as perform a search. To sort on a column item, or to change the sort order, simply click on the column heading.

Also in the List View are options just above the columns for New, Edit, Delete, and the icon to move up a level. The items in the New and Edit drop-down lists change depending on where you have browsed. You can also see other options next to these. For example, if you are looking at a list of workstations you see the option for Action. However, if you are looking at a list of reports, you see the item for Generate. Remember that some of these options are grayed out until you mark the check box next to a listed item.

**FIGURE 4.3**
Server List View.

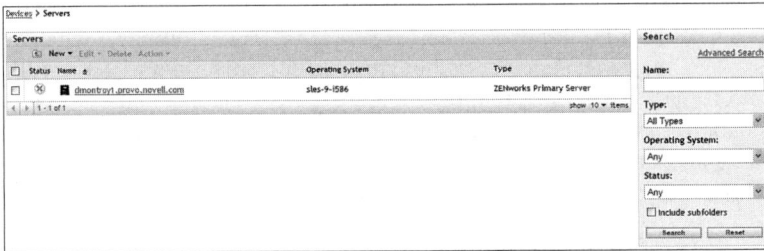

## SETTINGS VIEW

The Settings View enables you to change the settings for an object. For example, clicking on the word Advanced on the title bar for a snapshot takes you to the settings for that snapshot (see Figure 4.4).

**FIGURE 4.4**
Hot List Settings View.

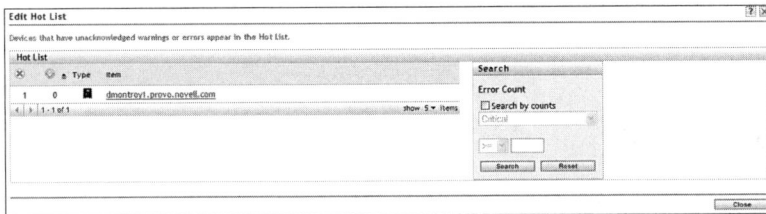

## WIZARD VIEW

The Wizard View enables multistep, or complicated, tasks to be accomplished step by step. One example of a Wizard View is the creation of a policy (see Figure 4.5). You can see more about creating policies and the steps needed by going to Chapter 9, "Policies."

**FIGURE 4.5**
New Policy Wizard View.

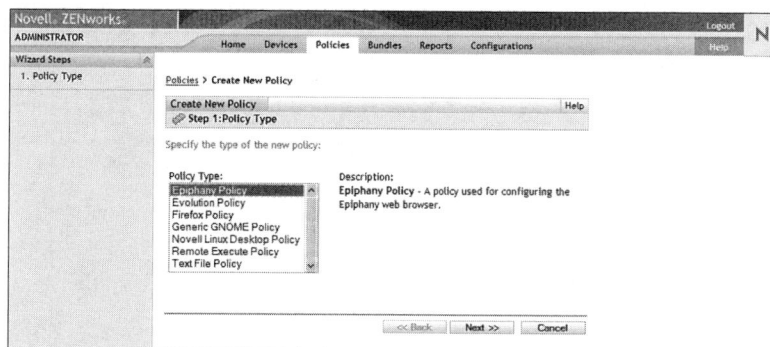

## Navigation Bar

Each view already described is coupled with the Navigation Bar. The contents of the Navigation Bar vary based on the Content View. For example, when you click on the Devices tab in the Banner, the top of the Navigation Bar changes to Device Tasks.

Some items in the Navigation Bar may always be shown if they are global. An example of a global item is the Frequently Used option. The items that display under the Frequently Used option are automatically built as you perform tasks. Your top ten frequently performed tasks are listed. The most frequently performed task is at the top of the list. Items in the list that are not used for five days are automatically removed from the list. The Frequently Used list is not customizable in this release.

## Object Browser

In some cases you are required to select multiple objects. In these cases, you are taken to the Object Browser. One example of using the Object Browser is to add a server to the Watch List (see Figure 4.6).

To select items in the Object Browser, either click on the arrow icon next to the item, or click Select All. To remove items, click on the delete icon next to the item, or click on Remove All.

**FIGURE 4.6**
Select Servers Object Browser.

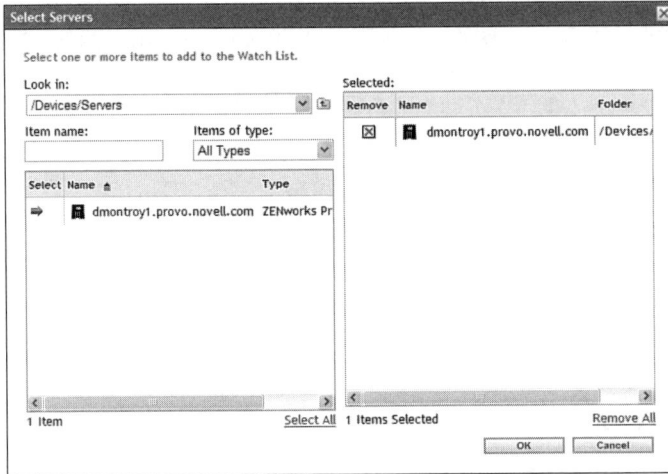

# Launching the ZENworks Control Center

You can launch the ZENworks Control Center through either Internet Explorer 6 SP1 (or higher) or Firefox version 1.0 (or higher). If you are using a browser that's not supported, you see a warning message when you log in. Enter the URL into the URL locator. The default URL for the ZCC is https://*server*/ zenworks, where *server* is either the DNS or IP address of the ZENworks server.

The first screen you see is the ZENworks Login (see Figure 4.7). Enter the Username and Password you assigned during the installation. You can also choose the Language. The ZENworks Control Center supports English, French, German, Portuguese, and Spanish.

Upon successful login, you see the Getting Started page (see Figure 4.8). From this page you can

- Get a product overview
- Learn how to register Linux devices
- Learn how to deliver an application
- Learn how to use policies
- Link to online documentation

**FIGURE 4.7**
ZENworks Control Center Login screen.

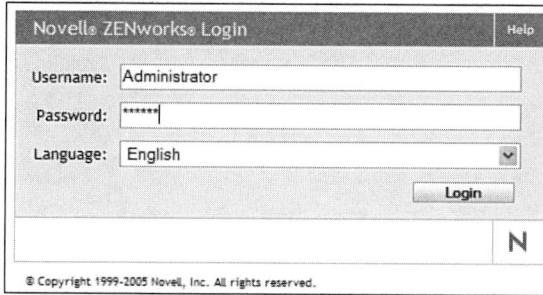

Hint: If you want the Getting Started page to come up every time you launch the ZENworks Control Center, uncheck the option Do Not Show Me This Again at the bottom of the page.

**FIGURE 4.8**
Getting Started page.

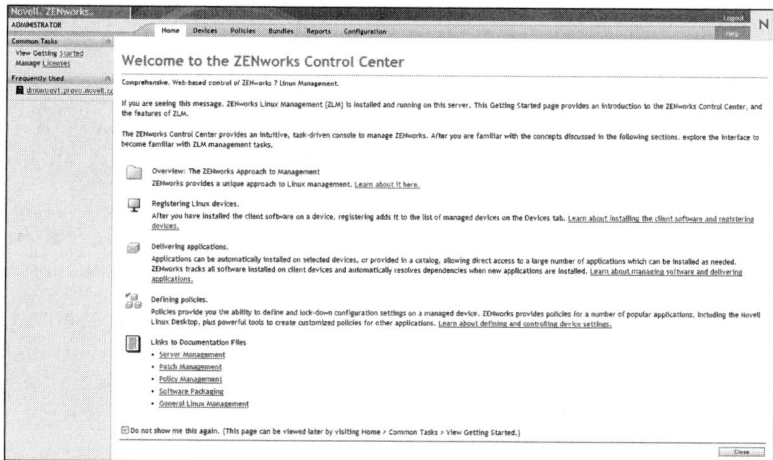

After viewing the Getting Started page the first time, you see the main home page (see Figure 4.9). This page contains important information about the state of ZENworks Linux Management.

**FIGURE 4.9**
ZENworks Control Center main home page.

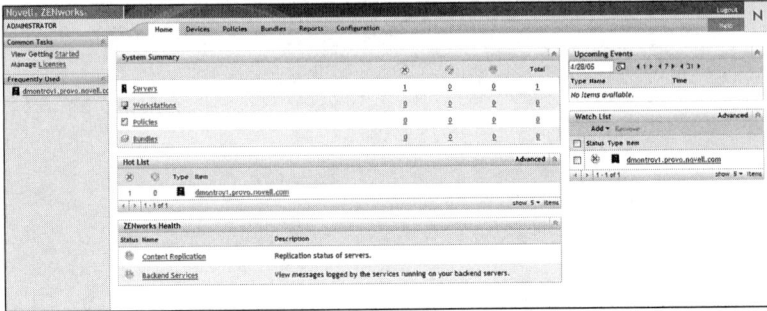

On the main home page you see five snapshots: System Summary, Hot List, ZENworks Health, Upcoming Events, and the Watch List.

The System Summary shows you the overall health of ZENworks Linux Management. You can see the status of the servers, workstations, policies, and bundles. Four columns across the top for each of these show Critical Status, Warning Status, Normal Status, and the Total. You can drill down to the status details by clicking on the underlined number. When you do so, you see the logs and messages for the status you clicked. You can then acknowledge the messages and they are cleared from the list.

The Hot List shows devices that have unacknowledged warnings or errors. You can edit the Hot List snapshot by clicking on Advanced in the title bar.

The ZENworks Health snapshot shows the health of the replication status of your servers, as well as the health of the backend services. If you see a Critical or Warning status, you can click on the underlined text to view the messages.

Upcoming Events displays events (policies, images, and so on) that are to occur on the date selected. The times the events occur for the specified date are also shown. You can change the date by typing it in manually, choosing the calendar icon, or clicking on the options to move to next day, next week, or next month.

The Watch List is a powerful tool for tracking the status of a specific workstation, server, policy, or bundle. This is especially useful if you have a workstation that has had sporadic problems or when you are applying an important policy and you want to know the status every time you launch the ZCC. To add an item to the watch list, follow these steps:

1. Click on the Add drop-down list.

2. Choose the item type you want to add (Servers, Workstations, Bundles, Policies).

3. Select the item(s) from the Object Browser and click OK.

Items in the Watch List remain in the list until you remove them.

# Navigating

You will find navigating in the ZENworks Control Center to be easy and intuitive. The controls and behaviors are similar to those you use for navigating a standard web page. Items that can be acted on are underlined, or the mouse cursor changes to a hand. A single left-mouse click is all that is needed to act on an item. I still find it funny to watch people double-click on items in a web page. Save your finger for more important things like dialing your cell phone for a pizza.

Hint: In some wizards or screens you have to scroll down to the bottom of the page to see the Next, Back, and other buttons. Running at a higher video resolution helps you avoid these situations. The ZENworks Control Center was designed to be run at a minimum of 800×600. We recommend that you run at a minimum of 1024×768 or higher.

# Searching Within a View

Some List Views also have an option to search. Searching is a powerful tool for finding information such as a specific workstation or server (see Figure 4.9).

Searching is done by entering the Name and in most cases Type and Status. You can also use wildcards when doing a Name search. For example, if you wanted to find all workstations that end in *finance* that are running Novell Linux Desktop, you would do the following on the workstation view:

1. Enter `*finance` in the Name field.

2. Choose Workstation from the Type drop-down list.

3. Choose Novell Linux Desktop from the Operating System drop-down list.

4. Choose Any from the Status drop-down list.

5. Click Search.

You can also perform an advanced search. This is done by clicking on the Advanced Search link in the top right corner of the Search box. In the advanced search you can choose the option to search with a filter in a report. This is a great way to leverage canned or custom reports to do your search. For example, you may want to search for devices registered within the last 24 hours. This is done by choosing that report and clicking Search.

The other option in Advanced Search is to create a new filter. This provides a lot of flexibility when searching. You can create either a New Filter or a New Set. Sets are groupings of Boolean searches. You can choose whether the sets are AND or OR by clicking on the drop-down list box next to Sets Are to Be. You can create multiple sets and filters by clicking on the New Set or New Filter text multiple times. Figure 4.10 shows an example of a complex search containing both filters and sets. If you want to delete a set or a filter, simply check the check box next to the one you want to delete and then click Delete. Notice that the word Delete is dimmed if no items are checked.

**FIGURE 4.10**
Advanced search using filters and sets.

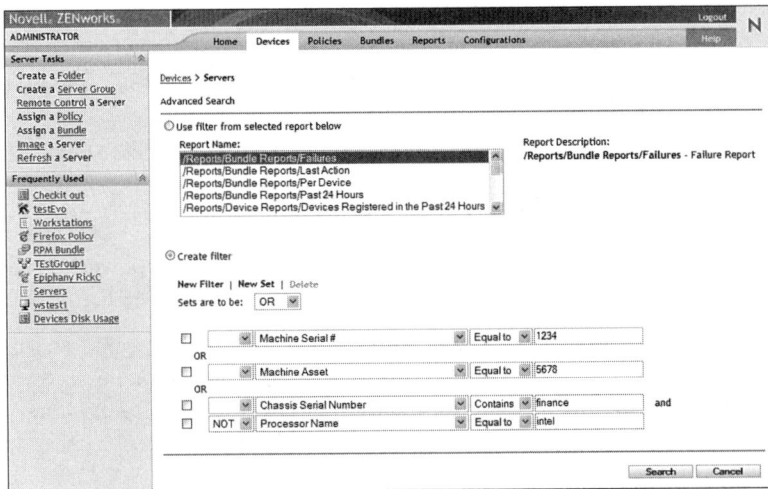

# Customizing the ZENworks Control Center

Every snapshot in the Portal View has a Minimize/Expand button on the far right side of the title bar. When a snapshot is expanded, the button displays two up arrows. In this state, the items beneath the title bar are visible. When a snapshot is minimized, the button displays two down arrows. In this state, the items below the title bar are hidden. The state of the snapshots is preserved as you navigate, or when you launch the ZENworks Control Center later.

# The Future

The ZENworks Control Center is a powerful tool for managing ZENworks 7 Linux Management. Future releases of other ZENworks products will also leverage the ZENworks Control Center for administration. This will enable you to manage Linux, Windows, NetWare, and Novell Open Enterprise Server with a single web tool.

# CHAPTER 5

# Registering Devices into the System

This chapter discusses registering devices in ZENworks 7 Linux Management. It primarily discusses two methods for registering devices:

- Manually through the command line
- Through the install

## Registration Keys and Registration Rules

After you have installed the ZENworks Linux Management server, you should go into the ZENworks Control Center and set up registration keys and/or registration rules.

Registration keys and rules tell ZENworks Linux Management how you want managed devices to be registered with the system.

### Registration Keys

Registration Keys are best used for situations where you want to create a limit on the number of devices that are registered. For example, if you know that a specific department has 10 workstations, you could create a registration key that is limited to 10 devices. As the devices are registered, you can easily see how many have been registered.

To create a new registration key, follow these steps:

1. Open the ZENworks Control Center.

2. Click on the Configuration tab.

3. Click on New in the Registration Keys Snapshot title bar and select Registration.

4. The Create New Registration Key Wizard starts, as shown in Figure 5.1.

**FIGURE 5.1**
Create New Registration Key Wizard.

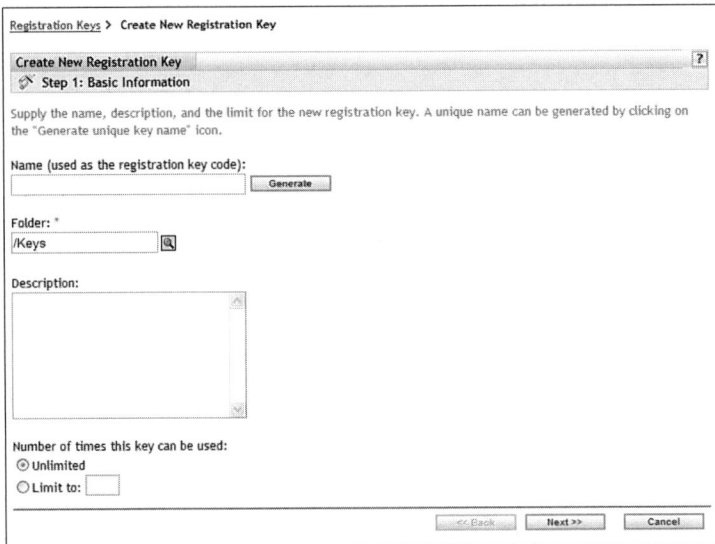

5. Enter the name for the registration key and specify the folder and the description.

6. Specify whether the key is unlimited or enter a number for the Limit To; then click Next.

   You then see step 2 of the wizard (see Figure 5.2).

7. Specify the rules for the name given to imported devices. You can choose several machine variables (HostName, CPU, DNS, GUID, OS).

8. Specify the folder where imported machines should be placed; then click Next.

   You will see step 3 of the wizard (see Figure 5.3).

**FIGURE 5.2**
Create New Registration Key Wizard, step 2: Naming and Containment Rules.

Registration Keys > Create New Registration Key

| Create New Registration Key | richard | ? |

Step 2: Naming and Containment Rules

Supply the template used to create the machine name, and the folder the machine should be placed in when imported.

Name given to imported machines:
${HostName}

Folder where imported machines should be placed:
/Devices/Workstations

<< Back    Next >>    Cancel

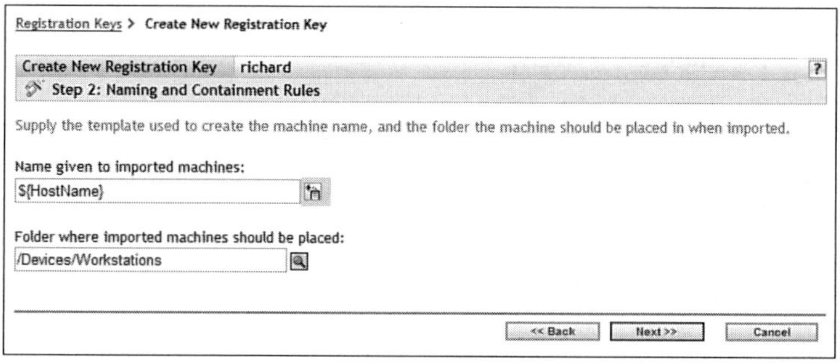

**FIGURE 5.3**
Create New Registration Key Wizard, step 3: Group Membership.

Registration Keys > Create New Registration Key

| Create New Registration Key | Richard | ? |

Step 3: Group Membership

Supply the groups new machines should be placed in when imported. Note: only groups that are valid for the folder selected in the previous step will be selectable.

Add  Remove

| | Name | In Folder |

No items selected, click add to select items

<< Back    Next >>    Cancel

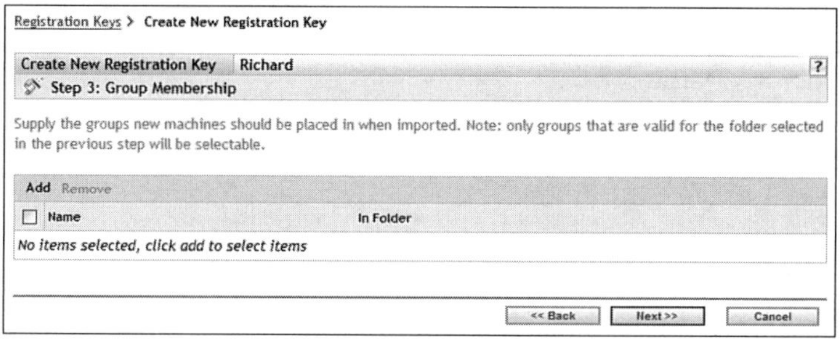

**9.** Click on Add to add the groups into which you want new devices to be imported.

**10.** Click Next to view the Summary (see Figure 5.4).

**11.** Click Finish to complete the wizard, then click OK.

You can rename, copy or move the registration keys by following these steps:

**1.** Mark the check box next to the registration key you want to modify.

**2.** Click on Advanced in the Registration Keys snapshot title bar.

**3.** Click on the Edit pull-down menu in the title bar and choose the option you want.

You can modify the general options of the registration key by clicking on the registration key name (see Figure 5.5).

**FIGURE 5.4**
Create New Registration Key Wizard, Summary page.

**FIGURE 5.5**
Registration Key Details page.

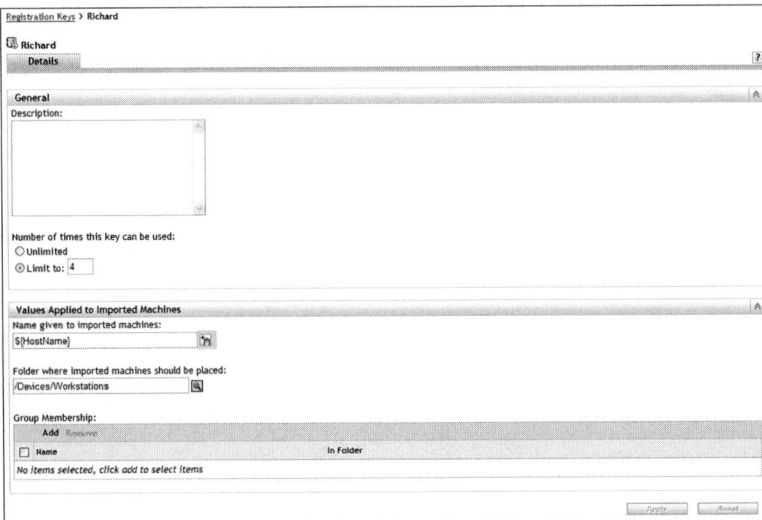

# Registration Rules

Registration rules are similar to registration keys. The main difference is that rules do not have a limit and you do not need to specify the rule when you register the device.

To create a registration rule, follow these steps:

1. Open the ZENworks Control Center.
2. Click on the Configuration tab.
3. Click on New in the Default Registration Rules snapshot title bar.
4. The Create New Default Rule Wizard starts, as shown in Figure 5.6.

**FIGURE 5.6**
Create New Default Rule Wizard.

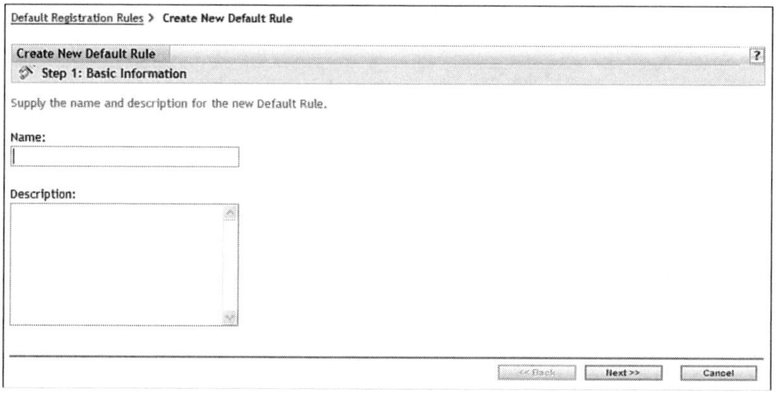

5. Enter the name for the registration rule.
6. Enter a description if you desire; then click Next.

    You see step 2 of the wizard (see Figure 5.7).

7. Click on Add Filter to specify the filters for determining which machines will use the rule. You must create at least one filter line.
8. Add to the filter by clicking on Add Filter again; then click Next.

    You see step 3 of the wizard (see Figure 5.8).

**FIGURE 5.7**
Create New Default Rule Wizard, step 2: Import Filters.

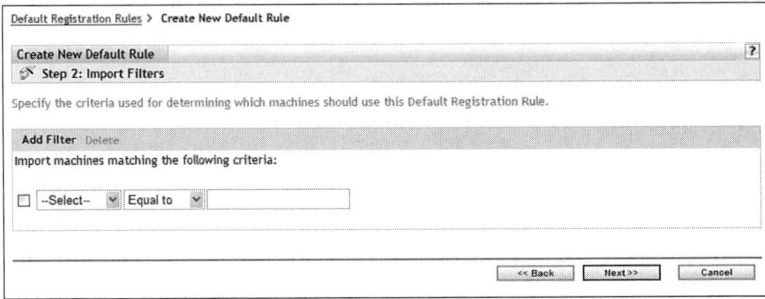

**FIGURE 5.8**
Create New Default Rule Wizard, step 3: Naming and Containment.

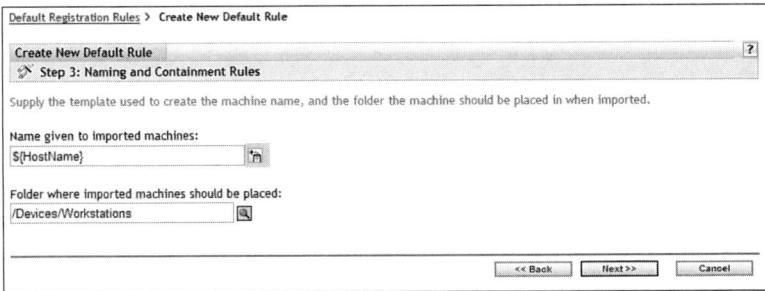

9. Specify the rules for the name given to imported devices. You can choose several machine variables (HostName, CPU, DNS, GUID, OS).

10. Specify the folder where imported machines should be placed; then click Next.

    You see step 4 of the wizard (see Figure 5.9).

11. Click on Add to add the groups into which you want new devices to be imported.

12. Click Next to view the Summary (see Figure 5.10).

**FIGURE 5.9**
Create New Default Rule Wizard, step 5: Group Membership.

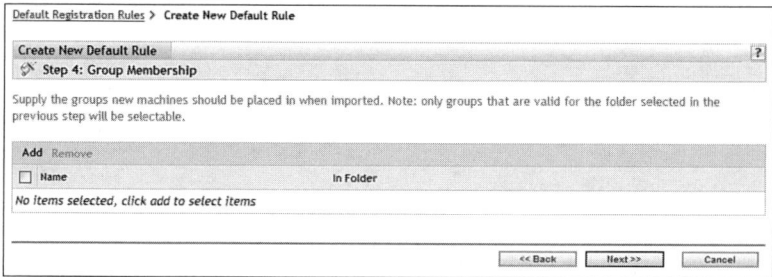

**FIGURE 5.10**
Create New Default Rule Wizard, Summary page.

**13.** Click Finish to complete the wizard; then click OK.

You can rename, copy, or move the registration keys by following these steps:

**1.** Mark the check box next to the registration rule you want to modify.

**2.** Click on Advanced in the Default Registration Rules snapshot title bar.

**3.** Click on Edit pull-down in the title bar and choose the option you want, or click Move Up or Move Down (see Figure 5.11).

**FIGURE 5.11**
Edit Default Registration Rules page.

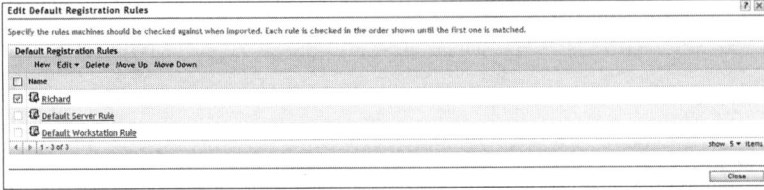

You can modify the general options of the registration key by clicking on the registration key name (see Figure 5.12).

**FIGURE 5.12**
Default Registration Rules Settings page.

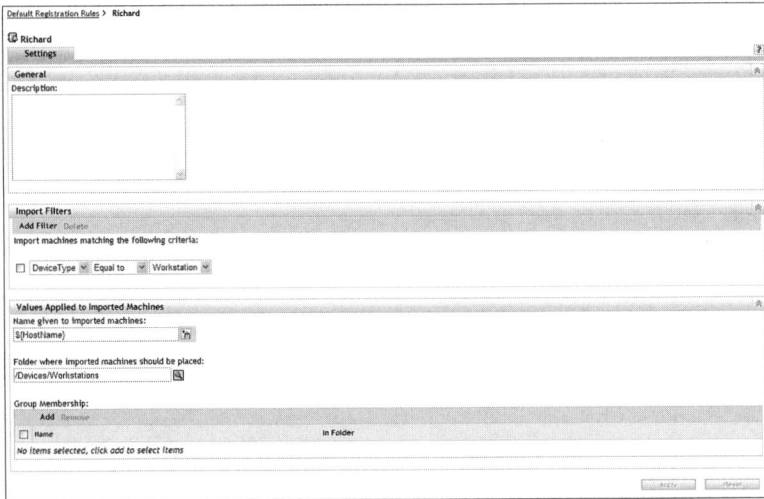

# Registering a Device

After you have set up your registration keys and rules as noted earlier in this chapter, you are ready to start registering devices. Throughout the ZENworks Control Center this is also referred to as *import*.

Registered devices can be either workstations or servers. Machines running Novell Linux Desktop are registered by default as workstations, and machines running SUSE LINUX Enterprise Server or Red Hat Enterprise Linux are registered by default as servers. This can be changed through registration keys or rules.

To register a device, follow these steps:

1. Log in as root on the device you want to manage and ensure that the ZENworks Linux Management agent is installed. Confirm this by using the following command:

   `/etc/init.d/novell-zmd status`

   This status should be identified as running.

2. If the ZENworks Linux Management agent is not installed, refer to Chapter 3, "Installing ZENworks Linux Management" and follow the steps outlined there under the section "Install the Client Software on Managed Devices."

3. Check to see whether the ZENworks service is running by typing **rug sl**. If it reports back ERRORL No services found, type **rug sa <servername>** or **rug sa <servername> -k=<registration key>**.

   The servername can be the IP address, DNS name, or URL. In this example, type **rug sa zlmserver.zendemo.com/**. You then see a progress bar showing percentage of completion for registration (see Figure 5.13).

**FIGURE 5.13**
Progress bar showing percentage complete.

```
zlmserver:~ # rug sa zlmserver.zendemo.com/

Adding ZENworks Service...
█████████████████████                                    33%
```

4. You should see a message that says Successfully added service. If you don't see this message, verify the servername and the registration key, make any necessary changes, and repeat step 3.

5. Verify the service by typing **rug sl**; you should see something like Figure 5.14.

**FIGURE 5.14**
List and status of ZENworks services.

```
zlmserver:~ # rug sl

# | Status | Type      | Name          | URI
--+--------+-----------+---------------+----------------------------------
1 | Active | ZENworks  | ZENworks Linux Management | https://zlmserver.zendemo.com/
```

There are additional options for **rug sa**. You can see these by typing **rug sa** **--help** or you can refer to Appendix A, "Commands," in this book.

# Removing a Managed Device

There may be a situation where you need to remove a device from the system. To remove a managed device, do the following:

1. Open the ZENworks Control Center.

2. Click on the Devices tab.

3. Browse to the workstation or server you want to remove.

4. Mark the check box next to the device and click Delete in the title bar.

   Following only steps 1–4 does not remove the device; you *must* follow the next steps as well:

5. Log in as root on the managed device.

6. Type **rug sl** to view the services. Notice that each service running has a number next to it.

7. Type **rug sd <service number>** to delete the service. Repeat this for each service. It is important to note that the services renumber each time you delete a service.

8. Verify again that all services are deleted by typing **rug sl**.

# Conclusion

Device registration is a powerful and flexible way to import the devices you want to manage. Before you begin registering devices, make sure you have a plan on how you want them to appear. This ensures that your devices are organized well, making it is easy for you to manage them going forward.

# CHAPTER 6

# System Settings

This chapter discusses configuring the settings in ZENworks 7 Linux Management. System settings control the behavior and configuration of ZENworks 7 Linux Management.

Within the ZENworks Control Center is a tab called Configuration. Clicking on this tab shows you a variety of options for controlling the behavior of ZENworks 7 Linux Management. The Configuration view has five snapshots: Administrators, Management Zone Settings, Registration Keys, Default Registration Rules, and Licensing.

## Administrators

The Administrators snapshot enables you to create new administrators, edit administrator attributes, and delete administrators.

The main administrator is always called "Administrator." This cannot be changed or renamed. However, you can change the password.

To create a new administrator:

1. Click on New in the Administrator snapshot title bar.

2. The Add New Administrator dialog appears on the screen (see Figure 6.1).

3. Enter the administrator name and password, retype the password, and click OK.

**FIGURE 6.1**
Add New Administrator dialog box.

**NOTE**

You can change the administrator password later by clicking on the name of the administrator, and then clicking on Change Password at the top of the navigation bar on the left side of the screen.

After you have created an administrator, you can further configure the administrator by clicking on the name. This takes you to the Administrator Configuration view (see Figure 6.2).

In this view you can

- Allow the creation of other administrators
- Allow the modification of Zone Settings
- Assign Bundle Rights
- Assign Device Rights
- Assign Policy Rights
- Assign Report Rights

To assign rights for Bundles, Devices, Policies, or Reports, follow these steps:

1. Click on Add in the title bar of the rights you want to change.
2. The Add Rights Folder dialog appears (see Figure 6.3).
3. Browse to the folder you want to modify.

**FIGURE 6.2**
Administrator Configuration view in the ZENworks Control Center.

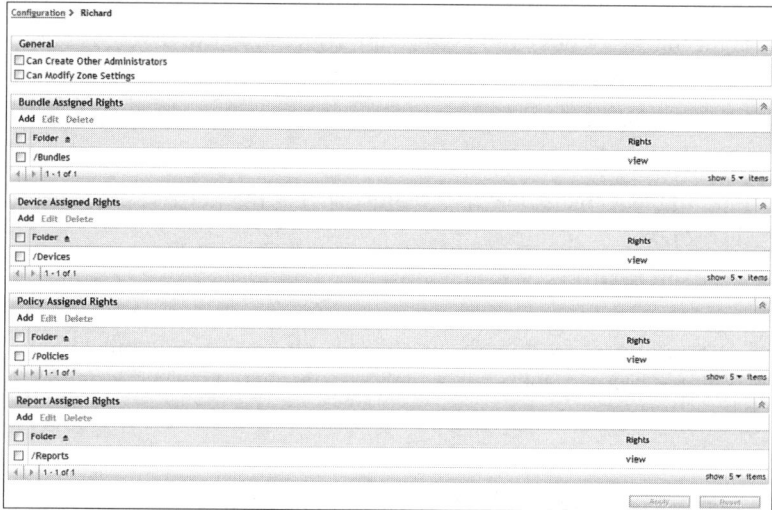

4. Choose the rights you want to assign (All, Modify, View).

5. Click OK to add the rights.

**FIGURE 6.3**
Add Rights Folder dialog box.

You can also rename or change the password of an administrator by following these steps:

1. Click on Advanced in the Administrators title bar.

2. Mark the check box next to the administrator you want to edit. The options for New and Delete become active.

3. Click the Edit drop-down list.

4. Choose Rename.

5. Enter the new name for the administrator in the Rename Administrator dialog box.

6. Click OK to make the change.

To delete an administrator, mark the check box next to the administrator, or check multiple boxes if you want to delete more than one. Then click Delete in the title bar.

# Management Zone Settings

The main part of the configuration page is the Management Zone Settings snapshot. These settings drive the behavior of the Management Zone. The Management Zone is the back end ZENworks servers and all the devices that are connected to those servers. You can read more about architecture in Chapter 2, "Understanding ZENworks Linux Management."

Within the Management Zone Settings snapshot, you can configure

- System Variables
- Refresh Schedules
- Device Inventory
- Local Device Logging
- Preboot Services
- Remote Management
- Centralized Message Logging
- Content Replication Schedule
- Platforms

You can easily determine whether or not an option is configured by looking at the Is Configured column on the far right of the snapshot. If an option is configured, the status is Yes.

# System Variables

System variables allow you to apply variables to all the managed devices.

To change the System Variables, follow these steps:

1. Click on System Variables in the Management Zone Settings snapshot. The System Variables page appears (see Figure 6.4).

**FIGURE 6.4**
System Variables settings page.

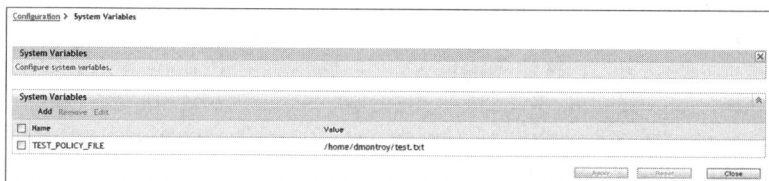

2. Click Add to create a new variable. The Add Variable dialog box appears (see Figure 6.5).

**FIGURE 6.5**
Add Variable dialog box.

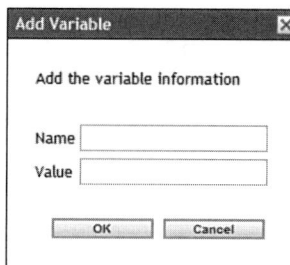

3. Enter the name for your variable and the value.
4. Click OK to add the new variable.

You can also edit a variable:

1. Check the box next to the variable you want to edit.
2. Click on Edit.

3. Make necessary changes.

4. Click OK.

To remove a variable or variables, follow this procedure:

1. Check the box next to the variable or check multiple boxes.

2. Click on Remove.

# Refresh Schedules

This setting allows you to configure how often, or the intervals, to refresh policies and settings for the Management Zone. Determining the right value to set
depends on the amount of devices, speed of your network, and the importance
of delivering policies within the Management Zone. We recommend that you
leave this setting as the default unless you are experiencing high traffic or poor
performance on your network.

To change the Refresh Schedules, take these steps:

1. Click on Refresh Schedules in the Management Zone Settings snapshot.

2. The Refresh Schedules content view appears (see Figure 6.6).

**FIGURE 6.6**
Refresh Schedules content view.

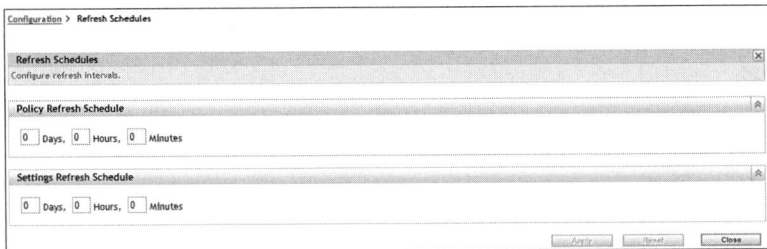

3. Enter the values you want for the Days, Hours, and Minutes for either
Policy Refresh Schedule or Settings Refresh Schedule.

4. Click Apply to change the settings.

If you want to go back to the default values, click the Reset button on
this page.

# Device Inventory

The Device Inventory settings enable you to configure the schedule for inventory scans and configure the rollup settings for hardware inventory (see Figure 6.7).

**FIGURE 6.7**
Device Inventory configuration view.

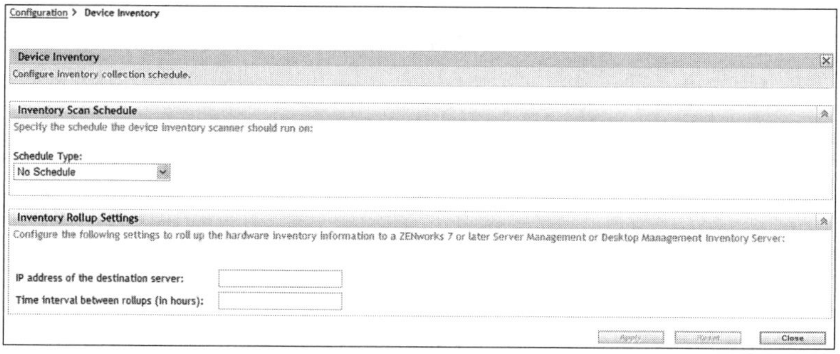

To specify the schedule for the inventory scan on a specific date, or dates, for devices in the Management Zone, follow these steps:

1. Click on the desired schedule type. The options include the following:

   - No Schedule
   - Date Specific
   - Day of the Week Specific
   - Monthly

   The various scheduling types are described in more detail in the following sections.

2. Select Apply to have the schedule applied.

# No Schedule Type

The No Schedule type prohibits the scan from occurring. This is the default schedule when the ZENworks Linux Management system is installed.

# Date Specific Schedule Type

With the Date Specific schedule type you can identify a selected date or dates in the year when you want this action to occur. When you select Date Specific, the screen displays the page shown in Figure 6.8.

**FIGURE 6.8**
Date Specific scheduling page.

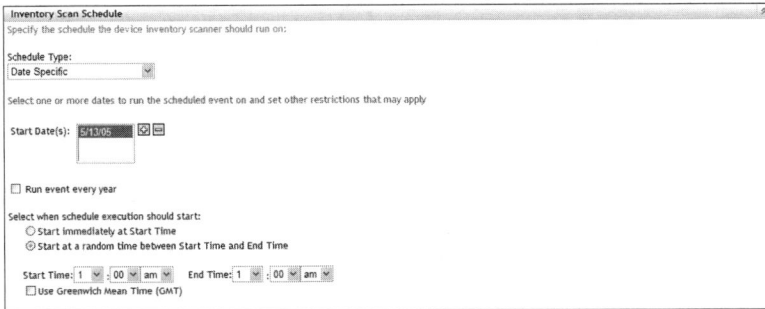

On the Date Specific scheduling page you may enter the following information:

- **Start Dates**—Press the plus icon. This brings up the pop-up calendar dialog (see Figure 6.9) where you can select the date you want. To change the month, click on the diamond next to the month. To change the year, click on the diamond next to the year. After you have selected your date, the dialog automatically closes and the selected date appears in the Start Dates list.

**FIGURE 6.9**
Date picker dialog for selecting a specific date of the year.

To remove the date, select the date in the Start Dates list and press the minus icon.

- **Run event every year**—Select the check box to cause content replication to occur every year on the selected dates.

- **Select when schedule execution should start**—In this area you can select whether the replication should occur at the given start time, or whether the execution should occur randomly between a given start and end time.

Enter the start time when you wish the replication to begin. Enter the stop time, if you selected that the execution should occur randomly.

Select whether the time entered should be interpreted as Greenwich Mean Time (or Universal Time). Otherwise the system assumes you mean the local time of the primary server.

# Day of the Week Specific Schedule Type

The Day of the Week schedule enables you to select a particular day of the week, along with some time schedules when you want the inventory scan to occur. Complete the following sections to identify your day of the week schedule. Figure 6.10 is an example of this type of schedule.

**FIGURE 6.10**
Day of the Week Specific schedule page.

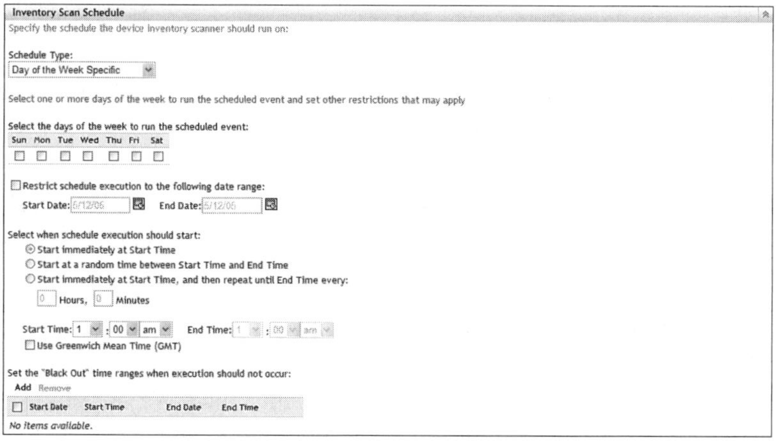

## SELECT THE DAYS OF THE WEEK

The first items to select are the days of the week when you want the inventory scan to run. Select the days of the week by clicking on the check box under your desired days.

## RESTRICT SCHEDULE TO THE FOLLOWING DATE RANGE

Select the Restrict Schedule check box if you want the system to perform the scheduled activity only during a specified calendar range. Then enter in a start and end date by selecting the calendar browse button and picking the date on the pop-up calendar view.

## SELECT WHEN SCHEDULE EXECUTION SHOULD START

This area is where you select the time or time range when you want the inventory scan to begin, on the days that you have specified earlier.

Choose one of the following options:

- **Start Immediately at Start Time**—This activates the inventory scan at the specified start time.

- **Start at a Random Time Between Start Time and End Time**—This choice generates a random time that is between the start and end times. Then the inventory scan begins at that randomly selected time.

- **Start Immediately at Start Time, and Then Repeat Until End Time**— This option starts the inventory scan at the specified start time. Then it relaunches the inventory scan at the interval specified in the Hours and Minutes fields. The system continues to scan at the interval specified until the end time is reached.

Next, specify your start time and end time. Do this by selecting the hour and minutes from the drop-down list and then choose either a.m. or p.m. Enter in both the start and end times.

Next if the time you have specified is a Greenwich Mean Time or Universal Time rather than the local time of the primary server, then check on the check box next to the Use Greenwich Mean Time (GMT) option.

## SET THE BLACKOUT TIME RANGES WHEN EXECUTION SHOULD NOT OCCUR

This option enables you to specify time ranges, which may fall within a calculated start and end time. For example, let's say that you like to do an inventory scan every Saturday of the month. However, at the end of each business quarter you want your servers working on end-of-quarter activities and not consuming cycles transmitting inventory data. You can do so by entering in your schedule and then selecting blackout dates for the end of each quarter. This way, if the calculated start time occurs within a specified blackout date, ZENworks does not launch the inventory scan. The inventory scan is not started again until the next scheduled time.

To enter in blackout dates, complete the following:

**1.** Press the Add menu item. A pop-up dialog box is presented (see Figure 6.11).

**FIGURE 6.11**
Pop-up dialog to enter blackout dates and times.

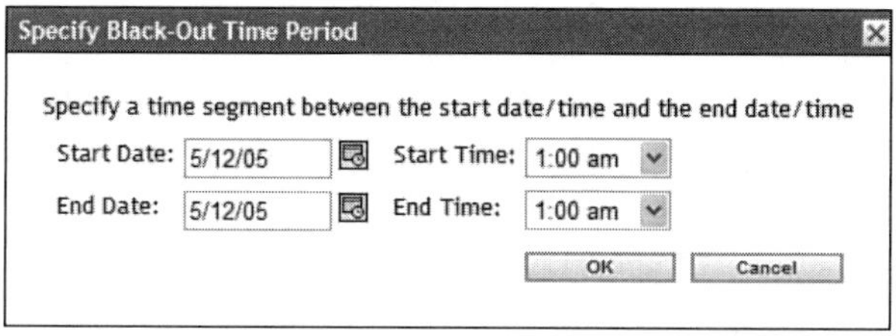

**2.** Enter the start date for the blackout period by selecting the calendar icon next to the Start Date field. This brings up the calendar pop-up, where you can select your date.

**3.** Enter the start time when the blackout period is to begin on the start date. Do so by clicking on the drop-down list next to this field and selecting a specific hour of the day.

**3.** Enter the end date for the blackout period. This is initialized to be the same date as the chosen start date.

**5.** Enter the end time when the blackout period is to end on the end date. Do so by selecting an hour from the drop-down list.

**6.** Press the OK button to have the time entered in as a blackout specification.

The entered blackout period is displayed on the screen. The blackout period begins at the specified time on the start date and ends at the selected end time on the end date.

To remove previously entered blackout periods, select the check box next to the listed blackout period and then click on the Remove menu item.

## Event Schedule Type

The event schedule enables you to select an event that triggers the inventory scan. Figure 6.12 is an example of this type of schedule.

**FIGURE 6.12**
Event schedule page.

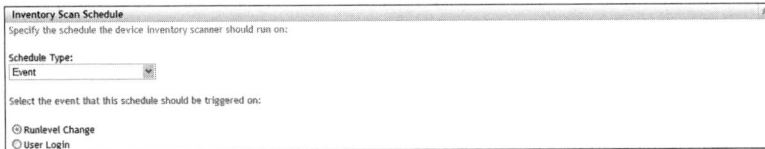

You can choose from two types of events: Runlevel Change and User Login.

When Runlevel Change is set, the inventory scan happens when the runlevel is changed on the machine. Runlevels vary from one distribution to the next, but there are some standard runlevels:

- **0**—Halt the system.
- **1, s, S**—Single user.
- **6**—Reboot the system.
- **a, b, c**—Process only entries in /etc/inittab that are marked with runlevel a, b, c.
- **q, Q**—Reread /etc/inittab.

You can find out the runlevels for the distribution by checking the /etc/inittab file for runlevels.

As you would guess, choosing User Login performs the inventory scan when the user logs in to the machine.

## Relative to Refresh Schedule Type

The Relative to Refresh schedule enables you to perform an inventory scan relative to a setting, policy, or bundle refresh. Figure 6.13 is an example of this type of schedule.

Choose one of the following Schedule Execution options:

- **Start Immediately on Refresh**—This starts the inventory scan at the same time as the refresh occurs.

- **Delay Execution After Refresh**—This option delays the start of the inventory scan by the specified days, hours, and minutes.

- **After Executing, Repeat Every**—This option causes the running of the inventory scan to repeat based on the specified days, hours, and minutes.

**FIGURE 6.13**
Relative to Refresh schedule page.

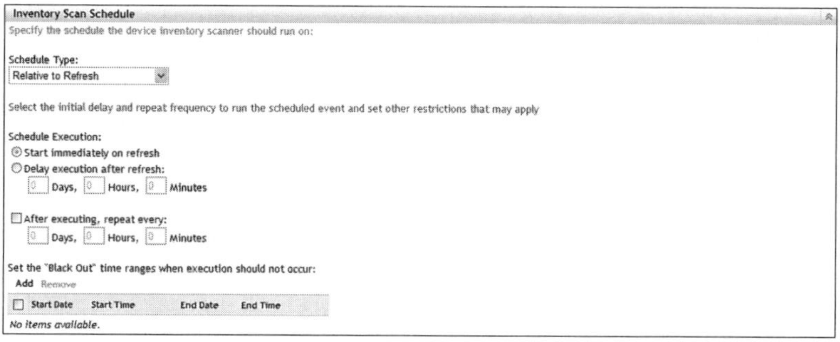

The Black Out option enables you to specify time ranges, which may fall within a calculated start and end time. If the calculated start time occurs within a specified blackout date, ZENworks does not launch the inventory scan. The scan will not be started again until the next scheduled time.

To enter in blackout dates, complete the following:

1. Press the Add menu item. A pop-up dialog box is presented (refer to Figure 6.11).

2. Enter the start date for the blackout period by selecting the calendar icon next to the Start Date field. This brings up the calendar pop-up where you can select your date.

3. Enter the start time when the blackout period is to begin on the Start Date. Do so by clicking on the drop-down list next to this field and selecting a specific hour of the day.

4. Enter the end date for the blackout period. This is initialized to be the same date as the chosen Start Date.

5. Enter the end time when the blackout period is to end on the end date. Do so by selecting an hour from the drop-down list.

Press the OK button to have the time entered as a blackout specification.

The entered blackout period is displayed on the screen. The blackout period begins at the specified time on the start date and ends at the selected end time on the end date.

To remove previously entered blackout periods, select the check box next to the listed blackout period and then click on the Remove menu item.

# Monthly Schedule Type

The monthly schedule enables you to select on which days of each month you want the inventory scan to run.

First select the Day of the Month when you want the process to begin. This is done by choosing one of the following:

- Start the scheduled event on a specific day of the month. This option starts the inventory scan on the given day of the month. Enter the numerical day of each month when you want the process to run.

- Start the scheduled event on the last day of the month. This option starts the scan on the last day of the current month.

Now select the time or time range when you want the inventory scan to begin.

Choose one of the following options:

- **Start Immediately at Start Time**—This starts the inventory scan at the specified start time.

- **Start at a Random Time Between Start Time and End Time**—This choice generates a random time that is between the start and end times. The inventory scan begins at that randomly selected time.

Next, specify your start time and end time by selecting the hour and minutes from the drop-down list and then choosing a.m. or p.m. Enter both the start and end times.

Next, if the time you have specified is a Greenwich Mean Time or Universal Time, rather than the local time of the primary server, select the check box next to the Use Greenwich Mean Time (GMT) option.

Now you can set blackout times for your inventory scan.

The Black Out option enables you to specify time ranges, which may fall within a calculated start and end time. If the calculated start time occurs within a specified blackout date, ZENworks does not launch the inventory scan. The scan will not be started again until the next scheduled time.

To enter blackout dates, complete the following:

1. Press the Add menu item. A pop-up dialog box is presented (refer to Figure 6.11).

2. Enter the start date for the blackout period by selecting the calendar icon next to the Start Date field. This will bring up the calendar pop-up where you can select your date.

3. Enter the Start Time when the blackout period will begin on the Start Date. This is accomplished by clicking on the drop-down list next to this field and selecting a specific hour of the day.

4. Enter the End Date for the blackout period. This is initialized to be the same date as the chosen start date.

5. Enter the End Time when the blackout period is to end on the end date by selecting an hour from the drop-down list.

6. Press the OK button to have the time entered as a blackout specification.

The entered blackout period is displayed on the screen. The blackout period begins at the specified time on the start date and ends at the selected end time on the end date.

To remove previously entered blackout periods, select the check box next to the listed blackout period and then click on the Remove menu item.

## Inventory Rollup Settings

This snapshot enables you to configure the settings to roll up the hardware inventory information to a ZENworks Inventory Server.

To change these settings, follow these steps:

1. Enter the IP address of the inventory server in the IP address field.

2. Enter the interval (in hours) in which you want inventory rollups to occur.

## Local Device Logging

This setting enables you to configure the warnings and errors that are logged locally on the managed devices within the management zone (see Figure 6.14).

At the top of the Local File snapshot you see the path to the local log file. This path cannot be modified. The path is **/var/opt/novell/log/zenworks**.

**FIGURE 6.14**
Local Device Logging page.

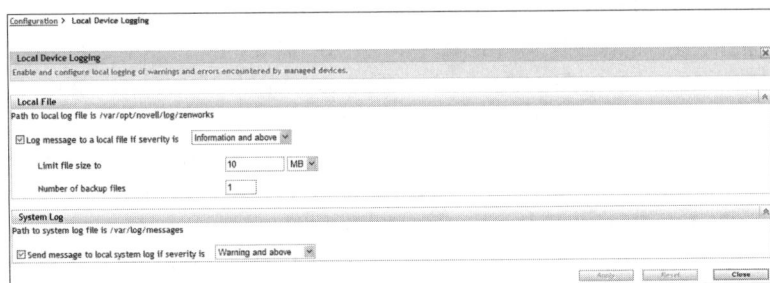

To modify the settings for the local file on the managed device, follow these steps:

1. Choose the severity of the messages you want to log by clicking on the Log Message to a Local File If Severity Is drop-down list box.

2. Choose Error if you want to log all errors. Choose Warning and Above if you want to log all messages that are warnings or severe. Choose Information and Above if you want to log messages that are informational, warning, and severe. Or choose Debug and Above if you want to log messages that are debug, informational, warning, or severe.

3. Enter the maximum file size to which you want the log file to get by typing in the value and whether it is MB or KB.

4. Specify the number of backup files you want to store.

5. Click Apply to have the changes you made take effect.

If you don't want to log any local messages, uncheck the Log Message to a Local File If Severity Is check box.

Just as you do with the Local File snapshot, you see the path to the system log at the top of the System Log snapshot. The path cannot be modified. The path is **/var/log/messages**.

To modify the system log settings, follow these steps:

1. Choose the severity of the messages you want to log by clicking on the Send Message to Local System Log If Severity Is drop-down list box.

2. Choose Error if you want to log all errors. Choose Warning and Above if you want to log all messages that are warnings or severe. Choose

Information and Above if you want to log messages that are informational, warning, and severe. Or choose Debug and Above if you want to log messages that are debug, informational, warning, or severe.

**3.** Click Apply to have the changes you made take effect.

If you don't want to send messages to the system log, uncheck the Send Message to Local System Log If Severity Is check box.

# Preboot Services

The Preboot Services configuration enables you to control the behavior of the preboot services when taking or putting an image on a managed device (see Figure 6.15).

**FIGURE 6.15**
Preboot Services configuration page.

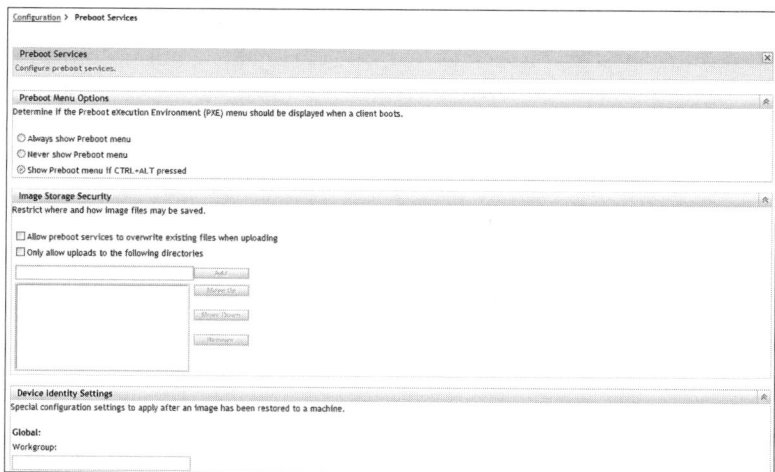

To specify whether or not to display the Preboot eXecution Environment (PXE) menu when a system boots, choose one of the three options in the Preboot Menu Options snapshot:

- Always Show Preboot Menu
- Never Show Preboot Menu
- Show Preboot Menu If Ctrl+Alt Pressed (this is the default option)

Unless the person using the managed device understands what to do when the Preboot Menu appears, it is recommended that you keep this at the default.

To restrict where and how image files may be saved, follow these steps:

1. Check the box next to Allow Preboot Services to Overwrite Existing Files When Uploading. Checking this option overwrites previous images taken from the managed device.

2. Check the box next to Only Allow Uploads to the Following Directories. This enables you to enter information in the text field next to the Add button.

3. Enter the directory path and click Add.

4. You can add more paths by repeating step 3, change the order of the directory paths by selecting the directory and clicking Move Up or Move Down, or remove directories from the list by selecting the directory and clicking Remove.

5. Click Apply to have the changes you made take effect.

Device Identity Settings are settings that add additional identity information to the device after an image is restored. Within the Device Identity Settings snapshot are three categories:

- **Global**—These settings apply to all imaged devices.

- **Per Machine**—These settings are specific to the machine that was imaged.

- **IP Configuration**

To apply specific configuration settings after an image has been restored, follow these steps:

1. Within the Global section, specify the Workgroup of which you want the machine to be part.

2. Enter the DNS Suffix.

3. Add servers to which you want to have the device connect by entering the server name in the Name Servers text field and clicking Add. To reorder server names, select the server and click Move Up or Move Down. Remove server names by selecting the server and clicking Remove.

4. Choose the method you want to apply for the computer name by selecting one of four options under the Computer Name heading:

- **Use Prefix**—Enter the prefix name.
- **Use BIOS Asset Tag**
- **Use BIOS Serial Number**
- **Do Not Automatically Assign a Name**—This option requires you or the user to manually assign a computer name after the image is restored.

5. Choose one of the IP Configuration options:

   - **Use DHCP**
   - **Specify Address List**—When you click on this option, you see the additional information shown in Figure 6.16.

**FIGURE 6.16**
Specify Address List information.

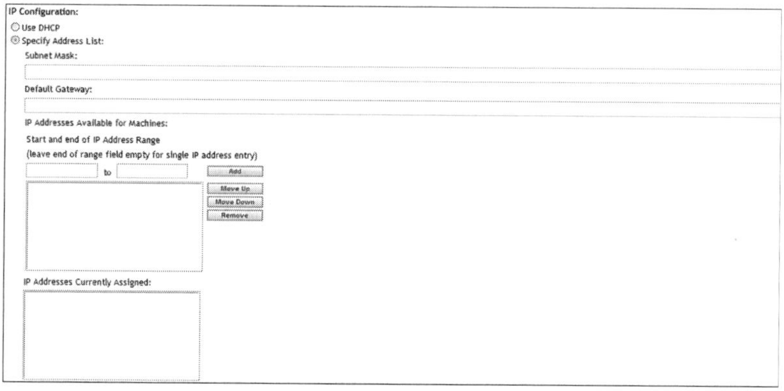

6. Click Apply to have the changes you made take effect.

To specify the address list, follow these steps:

1. Enter the subnet mask.
2. Enter the default gateway.
3. Specify the IP address range (start and end). If you want only one IP address, leave the End text field empty.
4. Click Apply to have the changes you made take effect.

You can add more IP addresses or ranges by repeating step 3. You can change the order of the IP addresses by selecting an address and clicking Move Up or Move Down. You can remove an address by selecting the address and clicking Remove.

The last field in this option is static and shows you all the current IP addresses that have been assigned. This is a great way to determine what IP addresses (or ranges) to use and the priority order in your list.

To determine which preboot bundle (see Chapter 7, "Bundles," for more details on bundles) to trigger based on the client hardware or the keys, follow these steps:

1. Click the Add button in the Preboot Work Assignment snapshot. This brings up the Rule Construction dialog box (see Figure 6.17).

**FIGURE 6.17**
Rule Construction dialog box.

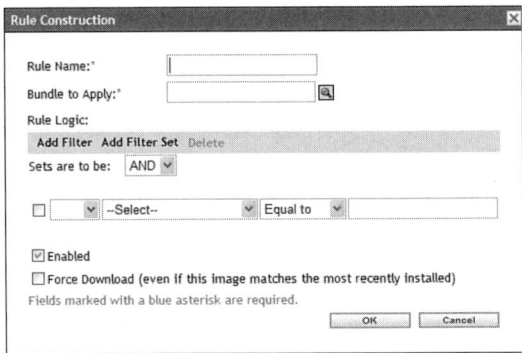

2. Enter a Rule Name.

3. Enter the bundle to apply or click on the magnifying glass icon and browse for the bundle.

4. Specify the rule logic by creating the filter. You can find more information on filters in Chapter 4, "Understanding the ZENworks Control Center."

5. Check the box next to Enabled if you want the Rule Logic to apply.

6. Check the box next to Force Download if you want to force the rule logic even if the image matches the most recently installed.

7. Click OK to create the rule.

8. After a rule is created, you can add more rules by repeating steps 1–7. Edit a rule by selecting the rule and clicking Edit. Change the order of the rules by selecting a rule and clicking Move Up or Move Down. Or delete the rule by selecting a rule and clicking Remove.

9. Click Apply to have the changes you made take effect.

It may be useful to assign multiple servers to handle imaging tasks. For example, one server could host the PXE services and another server could be used to store the image files. This is especially useful if you are imaging many systems at the same time.

To specify the servers that can host preboot operations, follow these steps:

1. Enter the IP address or DNS name of the server and click Add.

2. Add more servers to the list by repeating step 1. Change the order of the servers by selecting a server in the list and clicking Move Up or Move Down. Delete a server by selecting it in the list and clicking Remove.

3. Click Apply to have the changes you made take effect.

ZENworks Linux Management supports Intel Active Management Technology (AMT) to provide even more power when a device is being imaged. ZENworks provides the capability to store identity information and image identification on the device hard drive, enabling you to centrally manage when a machine should be reimaged. Intel AMT enhances ZENworks by storing that information on the AMT chip on the motherboard, allowing image management with network devices even when the hard drive is replaced. You can read more about AMT by going to www.intel.com/technology/manage/iamt/.

To enter the global AMT Enterprise names, follow these steps:

1. Enter the name in the Name List and click Add.

2. Add more names to the list by repeating step 1. Reorder the names by selecting a name in the list and clicking Move Up or Move Down. Delete a name from the list by selecting it and clicking Remove.

3. Click Apply to have the changes you made take effect.

# Remote Management

The remote management configuration settings are fairly straightforward. To change these settings, follow these steps:

1. Click on Remote Management in the Management Zone Settings snapshot (see Figure 6.18).

**FIGURE 6.18**

Remote Management configuration page.

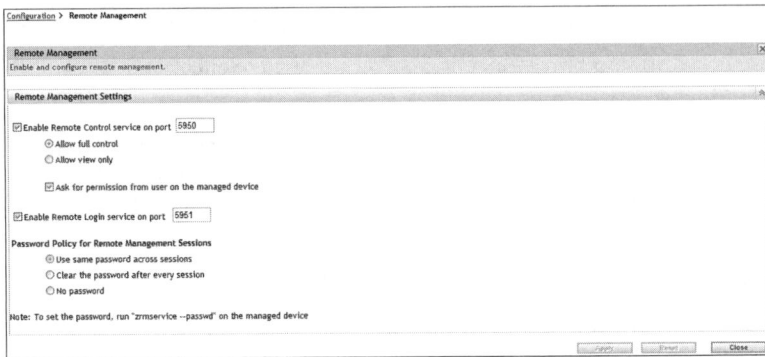

2. Make sure the boxes for Enable Remote Control Service on Port and Enable Remote Login Service on Port are checked. If they are not, you cannot control a device remotely.

3. Enter the port numbers for the remote control service and the remote login service. The defaults are 5950 for remote control and 5951 for remote login.

4. Specify whether you want to Allow Full Control or Allow View Only.

5. Check the box for Ask for Permission from User on Managed Device if you want to require that the user is prompted to accept a remote control session.

6. Specify the Password Policy for Remote Management Sessions from among the following:

   ■ Use Same Password Across Sessions

   ■ Clear the Password After Every Session

   ■ No Password

   You can also set the password at the managed device by running `zrmservice -passwd`.

7. Click Apply to have the changes you made take effect.

# Centralized Message Logging

You can change the settings related to logging by the central server by taking these steps:

1.  Click on Centralized Message Logging in the Management Zone Setting snapshot (see Figure 6.19) .

**FIGURE 6.19**
Centralized Message Logging configuration page.

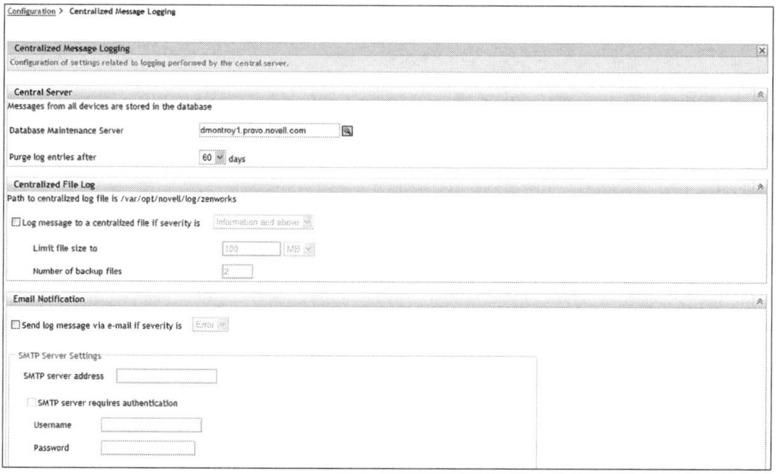

2.  Enter or browse for the Database Maintenance Server.

3.  Click on the Purge Log Entries After drop-down list box to choose whether you want to purge every 30, 60, or 90 days.

4.  Check the box next to Log Message to a Centralized File If Severity Is if you want to capture messages. Adjust the other options in this snapshot as you wish.

5.  Check the Send Log Message Via E-mail If Severity Is check box if you want to send an SMTP message to yourself or someone else when a specified message occurs.

6.  If you marked the option in step 5, enter the SMTP server settings for server address, and enter the username and password if the SMTP server requires authentication.

7.  Enter the message settings for how you want the email to appear. This includes the From, the To, and the Subject. You can use Format specifiers to further customize the Subject information.

8. Check the box next to Log to SNMP Trap If Severity Is if you want to send message via SNMP.

9. If you've done step 8, enter the trap target, the port, and the community string.

**NOTE**

This book does not go into detail about all the SNMP options.

## Content Replication Schedule

You can configure the refresh schedule used for replicating content between ZENworks servers by clicking on the Content Replication Schedule in the Management Zone Settings snapshot (see Figure 6.20) .

**FIGURE 6.20**
Content Replication configuration page.

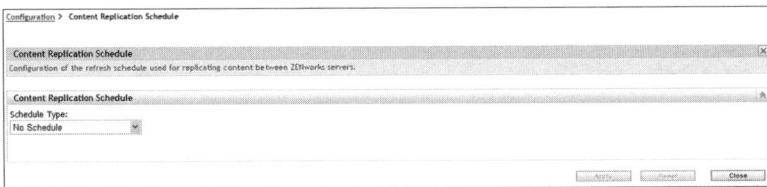

Details about content replication can be found in Chapter 13, "ZENworks Linux Management Database."

## Platforms

You can configure the available target platforms by following these steps:

1. Click on Platforms in the Management Zone Settings snapshot (see Figure 6.21).

A list of platforms is already in the view. These are the default platforms and cannot be edited or removed.

2. To add a platform, click on the Add button in the Target Platforms snapshot. The Add Platform dialog box appears (see Figure 6.22).

**FIGURE 6.21**
Platforms configuration page.

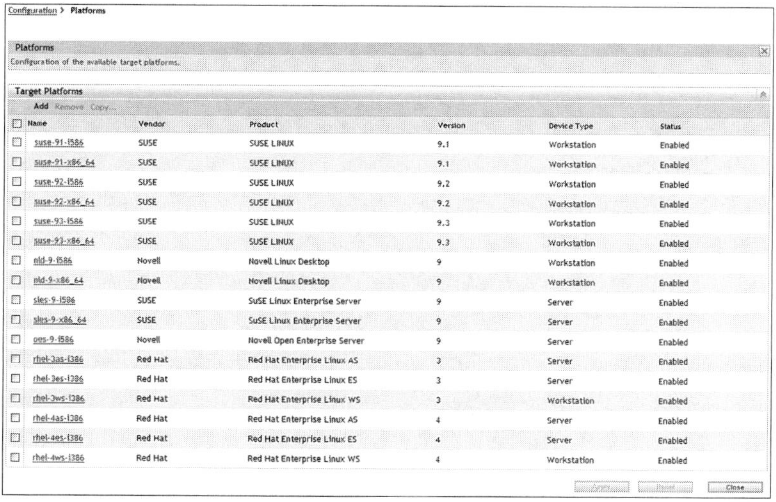

**FIGURE 6.22**
Add Platform dialog box.

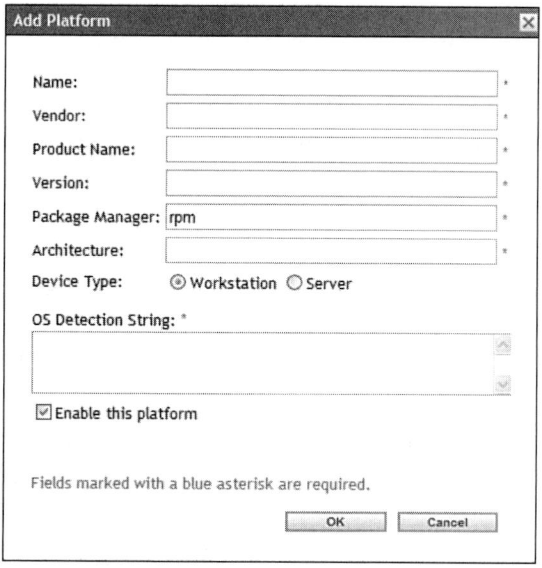

3. All the following information is required, as noted by a blue asterisk onscreen.

   - Name
   - Vendor
   - Product Name
   - Version
   - Package Manager
   - Architecture
   - Device Type
   - OS Detection String

4. Check whether you want this platform to be enabled.
5. Click OK to add the platform.

**TIP**

To simplify the creation of a platform, mark the check box next to the platform that best matches the one you want to add. Then click on Copy. This takes the information from the platform you marked and populates the fields in step 3.

6. Click Apply to have the changes you made take effect.

## Hierarchy and Other Places to Change Settings

If you are already familiar with ZENworks, you will understand how policies and other settings are enforced. However, if you are not, let's talk about what happens.

The configurations already covered in this chapter on the Configuration tab are "system" settings. This means that these settings apply to all the devices in the Management Zone. However, you can override the system settings by making the settings to a device group or a specific device.

To change the settings for a specific device, follow these steps:

1. Go to the Devices tab and select the server or workstation you want to change. You see either the workstation or server summary page (see Figure 6.23).

**FIGURE 6.23**
Workstation Summary page.

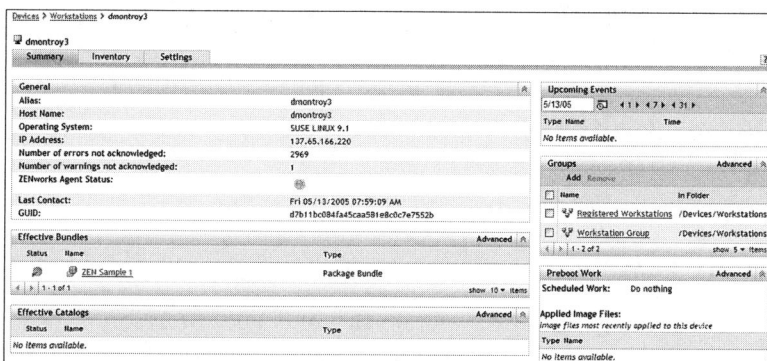

**2.** Click on the Settings tab to see a subset of the settings that are on the Configuration tab. These include

- System Variables
- Refresh Schedules
- Device Inventory
- Local Device Logging
- Preboot Services
- Remote Management

**3.** Click on any of these options and make the changes you want by following the steps in the earlier sections of this chapter.

If you followed steps 1–3 and made any changes, these changes will now take precedence over the system settings.

# Licensing

The bottom-right snapshot is called Licensing. This snapshot shows you whether you are running a licensed version of ZENworks 7 Linux Management or an evaluation version. If it is an evaluation version, you see a type of evaluation and you also see how many days are remaining in your evaluation period. Prior to the expiration of the evaluation, if you purchase the product, you can click on Change in the snapshot and then enter the correct product activation key in the Product Activation dialog box (see Figure 6.24).

**FIGURE 6.24**
Product Activation dialog box.

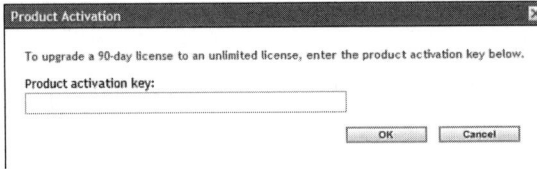

## Conclusion

Using settings is a great way to control many of the behaviors for the Management Zone. You can make system-level changes by going to the Configuration tab, or you can make specific device settings by going to the workstation or server pages.

CHAPTER 7

# Bundles

This chapter discusses bundles in the ZENworks 7 Linux Management product. Bundle creation, modifications, and assignments, like all administrative functions, are performed in the ZENworks Control Center.

## What Are Bundles?

Bundles are collections of content. This content can then be delivered to managed devices in the system.

Two bundle types are available in ZENworks 7 Linux Management: RPM bundles and preboot bundles.

RPM bundles are collections of RPM packages that can be assigned and delivered to a managed device. Each RPM package within a bundle may specify the architecture to which that RPM package is targeted. A bundle may contain any number of RPM files that are to be installed on the target device.

Preboot bundles contain a script or a reference to an image file that needs to be placed on a device. Additionally, you can perform preboot actions that take an image of a device at boot time and store that image on the server. A preboot bundle is delivered as part of the PXE system that can download an execution environment before the installed OS is launched on the target machine. The preboot environment can also be launched from a CD-ROM boot or from a locally installed ZENworks partition. From this environment, the system can deliver the preboot bundle without PXE.

# What Are the Advantages of Bundles?

Bundles are a good way to manage software collections. After a bundle is created, you can assign a bundle to a device and all appropriate RPM packages within the bundle are installed to the managed device. By using bundles you can group your RPM sets into logical entities that simplify the management of software delivered to your Linux systems.

# Bundle Groups

You may also create bundle groups. A bundle group contains an administered set of bundles and can be assigned to a managed device as one entity. So with bundle groups you can define bundle sets that should be managed and assigned as a single entity. Bundle groups may contain only bundles and not other bundle groups.

# How to Create an RPM Bundle

Complete the following steps to create an RPM bundle in ZENworks 7 Linux Management:

1. Launch a browser and enter the URL of the ZENworks Control Center.
2. Log in to the ZENworks Control Center.
3. Press Bundles on the menu tab at the top of the page.
4. Press the New drop-down menu and choose Bundle. This starts the Bundle Creation Wizard (see Figure 7.1).

Complete the wizard to create a bundle. The steps of the wizard are described in the following sections.

## RPM Bundle Creation Wizard: Bundle Type

On this first page you need to select the RPM bundle type to create. An RPM bundle enables you to specify a set of RPM files you wish to install on the targeted device. Select the RPM bundle type. Press Next. This moves you to step 2 of the wizard.

**FIGURE 7.1**
Step 1 of Bundle Creation Wizard.

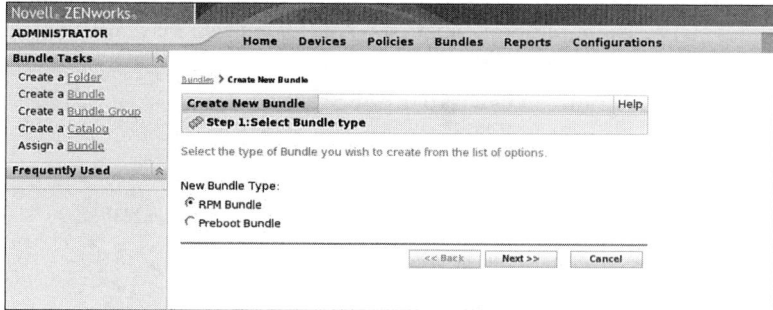

## RPM Bundle Creation Wizard: Bundle Naming

Figure 7.2 displays step 2 of the wizard.

**FIGURE 7.2**
Step 2 of Bundle Creation Wizard.

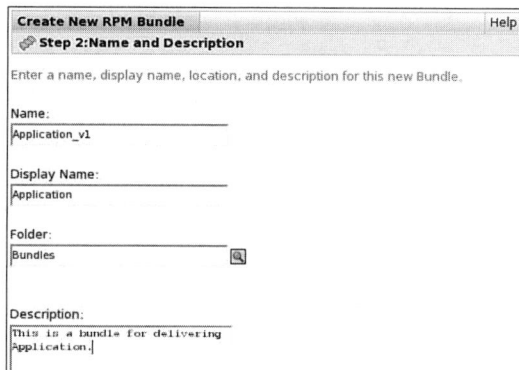

During step 2 of the wizard you must enter the following information:

- **Name**—Enter the bundle's name. This is the name that will be displayed in the ZENworks Control Center for this bundle.

- **Display Name**—Enter the name of the bundle that should be displayed on the end-user interface system.

- **Folder**—Browse to the folder under the Bundles area where you want this bundle to be created. Folders help you organize your sets of bundles.

- **Description**—Enter a text description if you wish. This description is used to assist you in remembering what this bundle may contain.

Press Next. This advances the wizard to step 3, where you specify the RPM files.

## RPM Bundle Creation Wizard: RPM Additions

Step 3 displays a screen similar to Figure 7.3.

**FIGURE 7.3**
Step 3 of Bundle Creation Wizard, to insert RPM files.

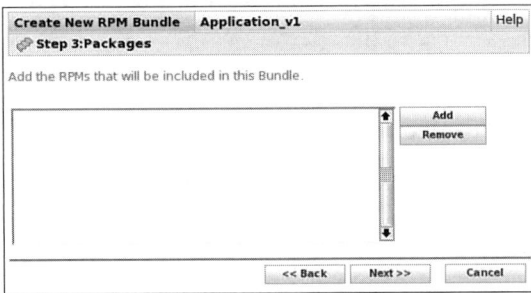

On step 3 of the wizard you are asked to enter each of the RPMs that you want to include as part of the bundle. Complete the following for each RPM file you want to include:

1. Press the Add button. This brings up an RPM File Upload file browser dialog (see Figure 7.4).

2. Select each of the following:

   - **Target Platform**—Select the target platform for the specific RPM. You can have several different target platforms in the same bundle.

   - **Install type**—Auto-Detect, Update, or Install.

     The Install option signals to the system to perform a parallel installation. Parallel installation requires that there be no file conflicts between the packages installed in parallel. This option is useful for kernels almost exclusively.

**FIGURE 7.4**
RPM File Upload dialog.

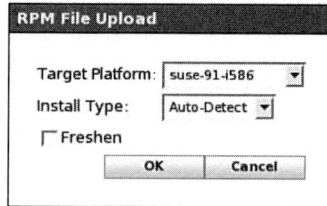

The Update option installs the package if it is not found, or performs an update if a previous version of the package is found on the device. The update option works in most cases because you do not have to worry about whether a package is on the device. The option always makes sure that it is.

The Auto-Detect method determines whether the package is applied with the Install or Update methods. Any kernel packages are marked Install and all other packages are marked as Update.

- **Freshen**—Select the Freshen check box if you want to install the package only if a previous version of the package already exists on the device.

**3.** Press OK.

**4.** In the next dialog browse to and select the RPM file that you want to upload. Press OK. This uploads the selected RPM to the ZENworks server and includes the RPM into the RPM list in the bundle. Continue to do this until all the desired RPMs are in the list. You may remove an RPM by selecting the RPM file and pressing the Remove button. After you have completed your list, press Next.

**NOTE**

If you have a lot of RPMs to place into a bundle, you may want to use the z1man command-line tool, which provides for the creation and insertion of wildcard-matching RPM files into bundles. See Appendix A, "Commands," for more information on the z1man command.

This takes you to the next page of the creation wizard.

# RPM Bundle Creation Wizard: Icon Specification

Step 4 of the wizard enables you to specify an icon file that contains the graphical icon you want to associate with this bundle. This icon is displayed on the target device when the bundle is presented in the GUI interface, which allows for manual updates.

When you enter or browse to the path of the icon file and press Next, ZENworks uploads that file into the system. After the icon file is specified, you move to the next step of the wizard.

# RPM Bundle Creation Wizard: Launch Scripts

Step 5 of the wizard enables you to specify scripts that you may want to run before the bundle is distributed to the device and after the distribution is completed.

You are first presented with a screen that lets you activate a pre-launched and/or a post-launched script (see Figure 7.5) .

**FIGURE 7.5**
Activation screen of pre-launch and post-launch scripts.

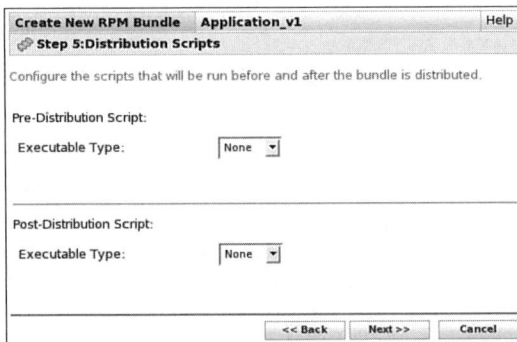

You can specify four types of script options:

- **Script**—This represents a shell script that can be executed on the managed device.

- **Binary**—This represents an executable program that can be run on the managed device.

- **Java**—This represents a Java executable class that can be launched on the managed device.

- **None**—This signals that you want no script to be executed.

The following describes how to enter into the system each of the Script, Binary, or Java types.

After you have finished entering your distribution scripts, press Next.

## SHELL SCRIPT

When you select that the script is to be a shell script, additional information fields are displayed, as shown in Figure 7.6.

**FIGURE 7.6**
Additional field for scripts of type Script.

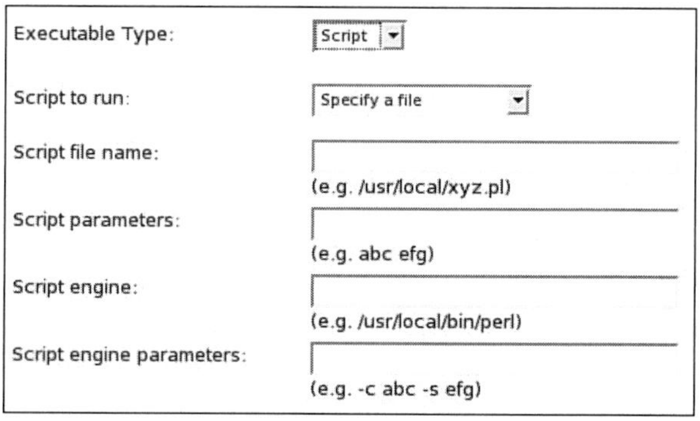

| Executable Type: | Script ▾ |
|---|---|
| Script to run: | Specify a file ▾ |
| Script file name: | |
| | (e.g. /usr/local/xyz.pl) |
| Script parameters: | |
| | (e.g. abc efg) |
| Script engine: | |
| | (e.g. /usr/local/bin/perl) |
| Script engine parameters: | |
| | (e.g. -c abc -s efg) |

The first field enables you to describe whether the script is a specified file already on the device (Specify a File), or whether the script is one you want to enter into the ZENworks Control Center (Define Your Own Script).

If you choose to define your own script, you are presented with a large text field where you can type in your script. This entered script is delivered to the managed device as part of the RPM bundle and executed in the standard device shell environment. There are no additional fields to provide to ZENworks.

If, however, you choose to specify a file, you need to enter data into the following fields:

- **Script File Name**—This is the path to the script file on the target device.
- **Script Parameters**—Here you identify any additional parameters you want to place on the command line after the script filename is specified. This results in parameters being passed to your executable script.
- **Script Engine**—This enables you to specify the interpreter that is to be launched to run your script.
- **Script Engine Parameters**—This enables you to specify any parameters you want included on the command line when the script engine is launched.

After all the appropriate fields are specified, the script is defined.

## BINARY SCRIPT

If you chose to have a binary script, the fields displayed in Figure 7.7 are presented.

**FIGURE 7.7**
Fields presented when a binary script is selected.

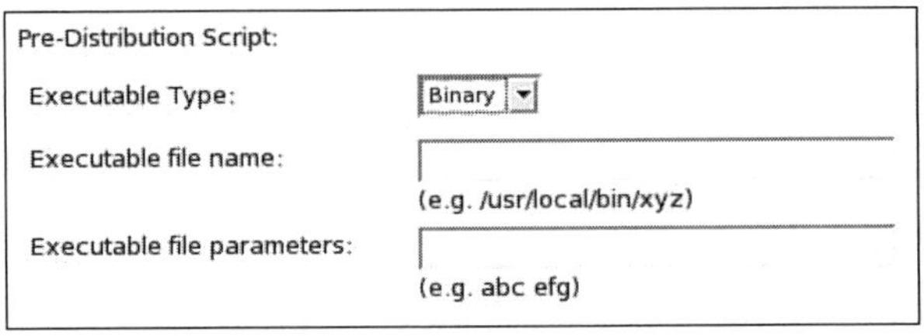

```
Pre-Distribution Script:

Executable Type:            [Binary ▼]

Executable file name:       [                    ]
                            (e.g. /usr/local/bin/xyz)

Executable file parameters: [                    ]
                            (e.g. abc efg)
```

Complete the following fields:

- **Executable File Name**—Specify the path to the executable file. This file must already exist on the managed device.
- **Executable File Parameters**—Specify any parameters you want to have included on the command line when the executable file is launched.

After these fields are specified, the binary script is defined.

## JAVA SCRIPT

If you chose to have a Java script, the fields displayed in Figure 7.8 are presented.

**FIGURE 7.8**
Fields presented when a Java script is selected.

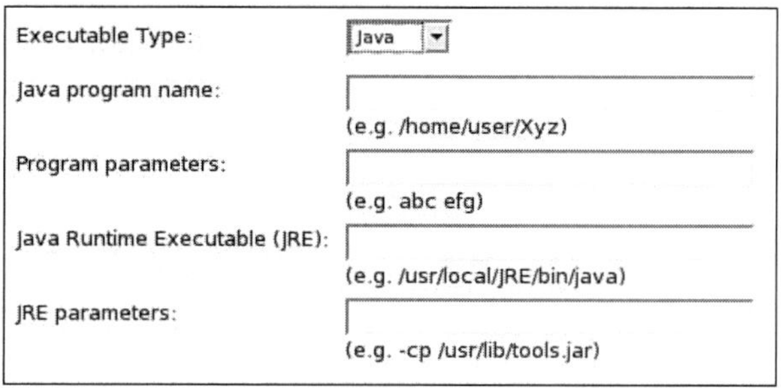

| | |
|---|---|
| Executable Type: | Java ▾ |
| Java program name: | |
| | (e.g. /home/user/Xyz) |
| Program parameters: | |
| | (e.g. abc efg) |
| Java Runtime Executable (JRE): | |
| | (e.g. /usr/local/JRE/bin/java) |
| JRE parameters: | |
| | (e.g. -cp /usr/lib/tools.jar) |

Complete the following fields:

- **Java Program Name**—Enter the class path to the class file that you want to launch.

- **Program Parameters**—Enter any parameters you want passed to the Java class at execution time.

- **Java Runtime Executable (JRE)**—Enter the path to the JRE that will be used to launch the class. The JRE must have been previously installed on the target device.

- **JRE Parameters**—Enter any parameters you want passed to the JRE system.

After these fields are specified, the Java script is defined.

## RPM Bundle Creation Wizard: Install Scripts

This step of the wizard enables you to specify scripts that should be launched before and after the RPM bundles are installed. Follow the same instructions as specified in the earlier Launch Script section to create the desired script.

After the scripts are defined, press Next.

## RPM Bundle Creation Wizard: Summary

The final step of the wizard is the summary page. The summary page displays all aspects of the bundle.

Review the summary page and press Back to return to a previous page to make changes, press Cancel to terminate the bundle creation, or press Finish to complete and create the bundle.

After you press the Finish button, the ZENworks Control Center displays whether the bundle was successfully created. Press OK to return to the ZENworks Control Center.

# How to Create a Preboot Bundle

Preboot bundles are associated with ZENworks imaging and make it possible to take or deliver an image to a managed device.

A preboot bundle requires that you take two steps to apply the image to the device. The extra steps are there to ensure that you really want that action to take place on the device. All preboot bundles may result in actions that destroy the data on the drive as part of the imaging process.

The first step involves creating and assigning a bundle to a device. In the second step you either launch the Perform the Preboot Task action or edit the preboot work snapshot on the device summary page.

Complete the following steps to create a Preboot bundle in ZENworks 7 Linux Management:

1. Launch a browser and enter the URL of the ZENworks Control Center.
2. Log in to the ZENworks Control Center.
3. Press Bundles on the menu bar at the top of the page.
4. Press the New drop-down menu and choose Bundle. This starts the Bundle Creation Wizard (refer to Figure 7.1).

Complete the wizard to create the preboot bundle. The steps of the wizard are described in the following sections.

## Preboot Bundle Creation Wizard: Bundle Type

On this first page you need to select the preboot bundle type to create. Press Next. This moves you to the next step of the wizard.

## Preboot Bundle Creation Wizard: Preboot Type

Figure 7.9 displays the following step of the wizard.

**FIGURE 7.9**
Step 2 of Preboot Bundle Creation Wizard.

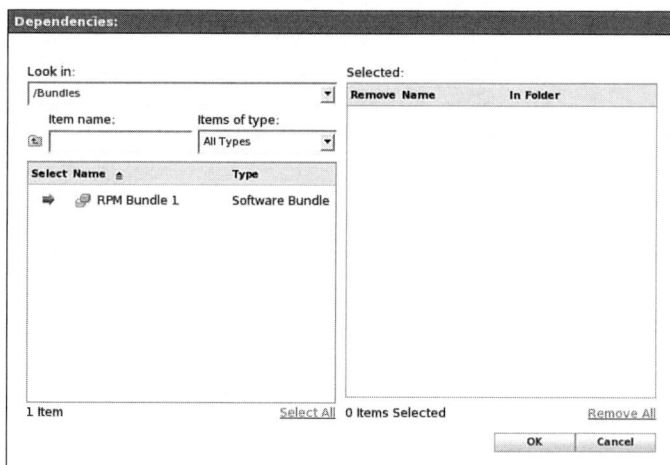

During this step you must select the type of preboot bundle you want to create. Select one of the following types:

- **AutoYAST Bundle**—This enables you to specify the parameters required to launch an AutoYAST automated installation of SuSE Linux.

- **KickStart Bundle**—This enables you to specify the information required to launch a KickStart automated installation of a RedHat Linux system.

- **ZENworks Image Bundle**—This enables you to specify an image that was previously taken with the ZENworks imaging engine. This image can be reapplied to any managed device.

- **ZENworks Multicast Bundle**—This enables you to specify that you want a ZENworks image sent to many computers in a single operation, using a multicast protocol that transmits the image only once over the network.

- **ZENworks Script Bundle**—This enables you to specify a Linux bash script that can be executed in the ZENworks Imaging environment on the managed device.

After you choose the type of Preboot bundle, press Next.

The following sections describe the wizard steps for each type of preboot bundle.

# AutoYAST Preboot Bundle Creation

The AutoYAST Preboot bundle represents a network installation of a SuSE Linux system onto the assigned managed device.

### AUTOYAST PREBOOT BUNDLE CREATION WIZARD STEP 3

After you press Next on the initial page, this wizard page asks you to name and place the bundle in your desired folder (see Figure 7.10).

**FIGURE 7.10**
General information page of Preboot Creation Wizard.

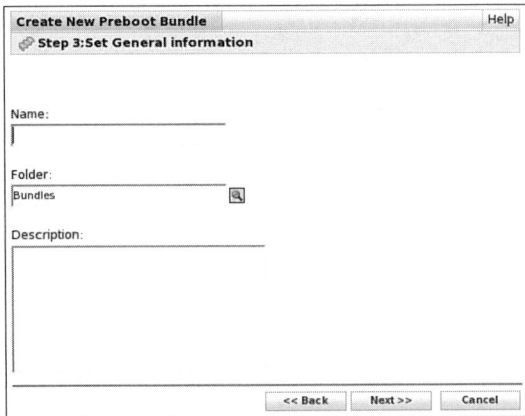

Enter the following information:

- **Name**—Enter the bundle's name. This is the name that is to be displayed in the ZENworks Control Center for this bundle.

- **Display Name**—Enter the name of the bundle that should be displayed on the end-user interface system.

- **Folder**—Browse to the folder under the Bundles area where you want this bundle to be created. Folders help you organize your sets of bundles.

- **Description**—Enter a text description if you want. This description is used to assist you in remembering what this bundle may contain.

Press Next. This advances the wizard to where you specify the location of the kernel files and other files for the AutoYAST process.

## AUTOYAST PREBOOT BUNDLE CREATION WIZARD STEP 4

In this step you must specify the path to the files necessary for the AutoYAST process. Figure 7.11 shows an example of this screen.

**FIGURE 7.11**
Bundle Wizard page creation of AutoYAST bundle, path files.

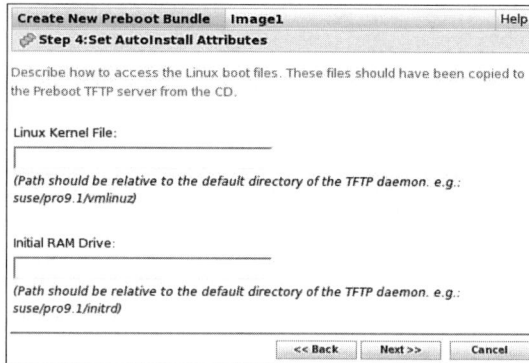

On this page enter the following values:

- **Linux Kernel File**—Enter the path to the requested Linux kernel file relative to the location of the TFTP directory on the ZENworks 7 Linux Management server.

- **Initial RAM Drive**—Enter the path to the RAM drive data file relative to the location of the TFTP directory on the ZENworks 7 Linux Management server.

Press Next to advance to the next page in the wizard.

## AUTOYAST PREBOOT BUNDLE CREATION WIZARD STEP 5

This step enables you to specify the protocol, server address, and path to the network install directory where your system can be found. Figure 7.12 shows an example of this page of the wizard.

Enter the following information into the page:

- **Protocol**—Select the protocol that should be used in contacting the Installation server. The choices of protocols are NFS, FTP, HTTP, or TFTP.

- **IP Address**—Next to the Protocol field, enter the IP address of the AutoInstall server that will be providing the installation information over the specified protocol.

- **Path to Install Directory**—Enter the path relative to the protocol where the installation directory is located.

Press Next to advance to the next page in the wizard.

**FIGURE 7.12**
Bundle Wizard page creation of AutoYAST bundle, AutoInstall Attributes for Install Directory.

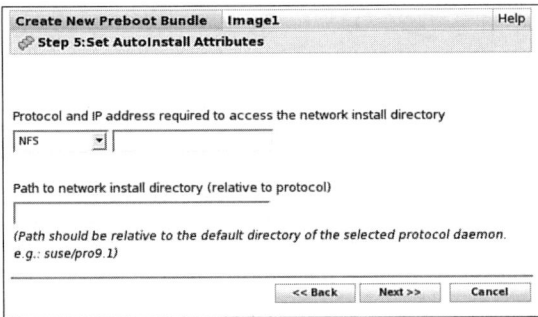

## AUTOYAST PREBOOT BUNDLE CREATION WIZARD STEP 6

This step enables you to specify the protocol, server address, and path to the AutoYAST script on your network. Figure 7.13 shows an example of this page of the wizard.

Enter the following information into the page:

- **Protocol**—Select the protocol that should be used in contacting the Installation server. The choices of protocols are NFS, FTP, HTTP, or TFTP.

- **IP Address**—Next to the Protocol field, enter the IP address of the AutoInstall server that will be providing the installation information over the specified protocol.

- **AutoYAST Script Name**—Enter the path and script filename of the AutoYAST script that is to coordinate your installation.

- **Additional Kernel Parameters**—Enter any additional Linux kernel parameters you want passed to the AutoYAST system.

Press Next to advance to the next page in the wizard.

**FIGURE 7.13**
Bundle Wizard page creation of AutoYAST bundle, AutoInstall Attributes for AutoYAST script.

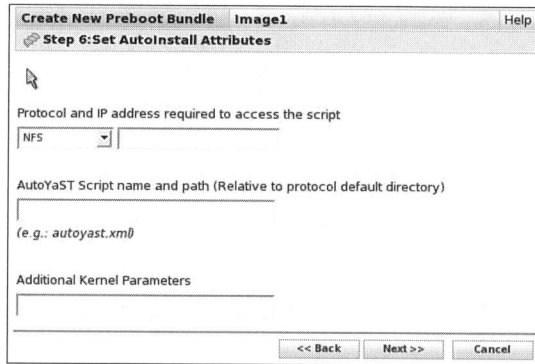

## AUTOYAST PREBOOT BUNDLE CREATION WIZARD: SUMMARY

This step in the wizard provides a summary of your Preboot bundle.

Review the summary page and press Back to return to a previous page to make changes, Cancel to terminate the bundle creation, or Finish to complete and create the bundle.

After you press the Finish button, the ZENworks Control Center displays whether the bundle was created successfully. Press OK to return to the ZENworks Control Center.

# KickStart Preboot Bundle Creation

The KickStart preboot bundle represents a network installation of a RedHat system onto the assigned managed device.

## KICKSTART PREBOOT BUNDLE CREATION WIZARD: NAMING

This wizard page asks you to name and place the bundle in your desired folder (refer to Figure 7.10).

Press Next. This advances the wizard to where you specify the location of the kernel files and other files for the KickStart process.

## KICKSTART PREBOOT BUNDLE CREATION WIZARD: PATHS

In this step you must specify the path to the files necessary for the KickStart process. Figure 7.14 shows an example of this screen.

**FIGURE 7.14**
Bundle Wizard page creation of KickStart bundle, path files.

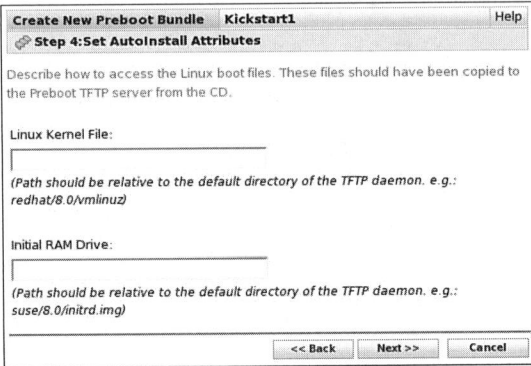

On this page enter the following values:

- **Linux Kernel File**—Enter the path to the requested Linux Kernel file relative to the location of the TFTP directory on the ZENworks 7 Linux Management server.

- **Initial RAM Drive**—Enter the path to the RAM drive data file relative to the location of the TFTP directory on the ZENworks 7 Linux Management server.

Press Next to advance to the next page in the wizard.

## KICKSTART PREBOOT BUNDLE CREATION WIZARD: SERVER

This step enables you to specify the protocol, server address, and path to the KickStart script on your network. Figure 7.15 shows an example of this page of the wizard.

Enter the following information into the page:

- **Protocol**—Select the protocol that should be used in contacting the Installation server. The choices of protocols are NFS, FTP, or HTTP.

- **IP Address**—Next to the Protocol field, enter the IP address of the AutoInstall server that will be providing the installation information over the specified protocol.

- **KickStart Script Name**—Enter the path and script filename of the KickStart script that is to coordinate your installation.

- **Additional Kernel Parameters**—Enter any additional Linux kernel parameters you want passed to the KickStart system.

Press Next to advance to the next page in the wizard.

**FIGURE 7.15**
Bundle Wizard page creation of KickStart bundle, AutoInstall Attributes for KickStart script.

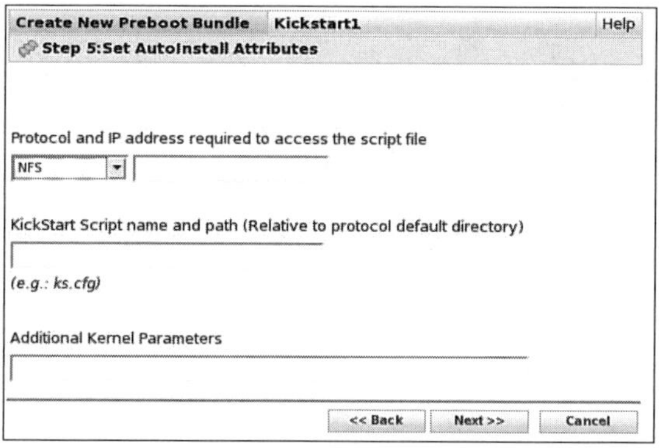

### KICKSTART PREBOOT BUNDLE CREATION WIZARD: SUMMARY

This step in the wizard provides a summary of your Preboot bundle.

Review the summary page and press Back to return to a previous page to make changes, Cancel to terminate the bundle creation, or Finish to complete and create the bundle.

After you press the Finish button, the ZENworks Control Center displays whether the bundle was created successfully. Press OK to return to the ZENworks Control Center.

## ZENworks Image Preboot Bundle Creation

The ZENworks Image Preboot bundle represents an image that has been created with the ZENworks Image Explorer or an image that was taken from an existing device and stored on the ZENworks server.

### ZENWORKS IMAGE PREBOOT BUNDLE CREATION WIZARD: NAMING

This wizard page asks you to name and place the bundle in your desired folder (refer to Figure 7.10).

Press Next. This advances the wizard to where you specify the base and optional add-on image files.

## ZENWORKS IMAGE PREBOOT BUNDLE CREATION WIZARD: IMAGE FILE

In this step you must specify the path to the image (.zmg) file that contains the base image and any additional add-on image files to include in the imaging process. Figure 7.16 shows an example of this screen.

When a ZENworks Image is placed on a system, the base image is first placed onto the drive. The placing of a base image is, by default, destructive and removes any data and partitioning that may have been on that drive. After the base image is applied to the device, the add-on images, which are never destructive, are applied to the disk drive.

**FIGURE 7.16**
Bundle Wizard page creation of ZENworks Image bundle, base and add-on files.

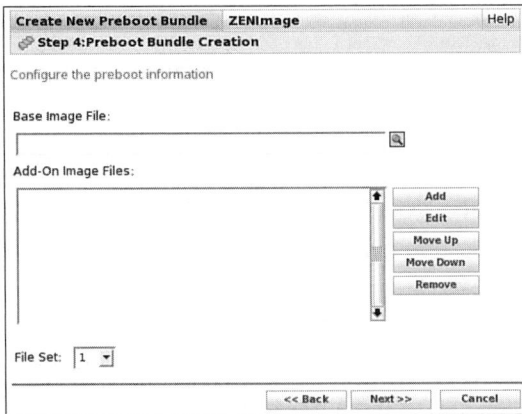

On this page enter the following values:

- **Base Image File**—You cannot enter any data into the specified field. You must press the Browse button to the right of the field. This brings up the dialog box shown in Figure 7.17.

  Enter the following information into the dialog box:

  - **Server Object, IP, or DNS**—Enter into the field the device name in ZENworks for the server that holds the imaging files. You may alternatively enter the IP or DNS address of that server. You may optionally press the Browse button next to the field and browse to and select the server from the ZENworks Control Center.

- **File Path on Server**—Enter the full path to the .zmg file that represents your base image.

**FIGURE 7.17**
Base Image File browse dialog.

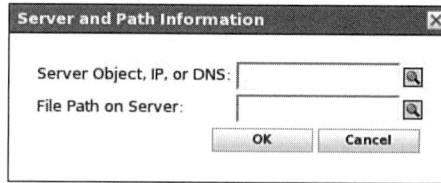

After you have entered these values, press the OK button.

- **Add-On Image Files**—You may optionally add Add-On image files to the bundle by pressing the Add button to the right. This brings up the same dialog to define the server and filename of the image file (see Figure 7.16). After you have entered your Add-On image files, you may remove, edit, or reorder the list by selecting the specific Add-On image file and then selecting the action from the buttons on the left.

- **File Set**—Select the file set out of the Base Image that you want applied to the device. The File Set enables the system to selectively place files out of the image onto the managed device.

Press Next to advance to the next page in the wizard.

### ZENWORKS IMAGING PREBOOT BUNDLE CREATION WIZARD: SUMMARY

This step in the wizard provides a summary of your Preboot bundle.

Review the summary page and press Back to return to a previous page to make changes, Cancel to terminate the bundle creation, or Finish to complete and create the bundle.

After you press the Finish button, the ZENworks Control Center displays whether the bundle was created successfully. Press OK to return to the ZENworks Control Center.

## ZENworks Script Preboot Bundle Creation

The ZENworks Script Preboot bundle represents a script that will be executed in the ZENworks Imaging environment on the device.

## ZENWORKS SCRIPT PREBOOT BUNDLE CREATION WIZARD: NAMING

This wizard page asks you to name and place the bundle in your desired folder (refer to Figure 7.10).

Press Next. This advances the wizard to where you specify the script commands you want executed.

## ZENWORKS SCRIPT PREBOOT BUNDLE CREATION WIZARD: SCRIPT

This step enables you to enter the script that you want launched. Figure 7.18 shows an example of this screen.

**FIGURE 7.18**
Bundle Wizard page creation of ZENworks Image bundle, script.

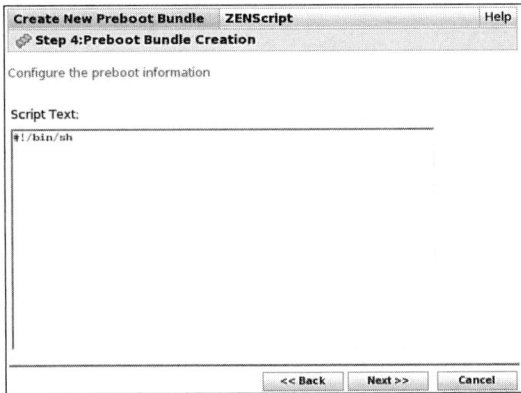

On this page enter the script into the text box.

Press Next to advance to the next page in the wizard.

## ZENWORKS SCRIPT PREBOOT BUNDLE CREATION WIZARD: SUMMARY

This step in the wizard provides a summary of your Preboot bundle.

Review the summary page and press Back to return to a previous page to make changes, Cancel to terminate the bundle creation, or Finish to complete and create the bundle.

After you press the Finish button, the ZENworks Control Center displays the success or failure of the bundle creation. Press OK to return to the ZENworks Control Center.

# How to Assign a Bundle to a Device

When a bundle is assigned to a device either directly or indirectly, ZENworks installs the RPMs in the bundle or applies the preboot bundle to that device.

A bundle that is newly assigned to a device is installed when the next bundle refresh cycle occurs. This can happen at boot time or based on the bundle refresh setting in the managed device's zone.

You can follow the following method to assign a bundle to a device. One method is as follows:

1. Open the ZENworks Control Center.

2. Click on Devices on the menu at the top of the screen.

3. Browse within the Devices folder to the folder where the specific device is located.

4. Select the specific device by clicking on the check box in the list next to the device. This activates the rest of the device menu.

5. Select the Action menu item to open the drop-down list and select Assign Bundle. This launches the Bundle Assignment Wizard.

# What Happens When a Bundle Is Assigned to a Device

When an RPM bundle is assigned to a device, ZENworks attempts to install the packages in that bundle on the device. When the device performs a refresh, which is done at boot time or when the scheduled refresh interval is reached, the device becomes aware of any newly assigned bundles.

Because of the destructive nature of a preboot bundle, it is not automatically applied to the device. Manual steps must be performed for a preboot bundle to be applied to the device. Take the following steps to cause the device to run the preboot bundle at the next boot:

1. Open the ZENworks Control Center.

2. Browse to the device that needs to run the preboot bundle.

3. Open the device to the Summary page.

4. Select the Advanced option in the Preboot Work snapshot. A sample of this snapshot is displayed in Figure 7.19.

**FIGURE 7.19**
Sample Preboot Work snapshot on a device's Summary page.

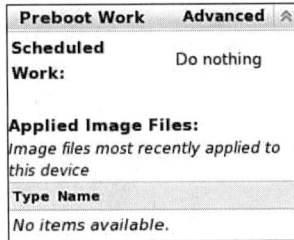

| Preboot Work | Advanced ⤢ |
|---|---|
| **Scheduled Work:** | Do nothing |

**Applied Image Files:**
*Image files most recently applied to this device*

| Type Name |
|---|
| *No items available.* |

5. The Advanced page of Preboot Work is displayed (see Figure 7.20).

**FIGURE 7.20**
Sample Preboot Work Advanced page.

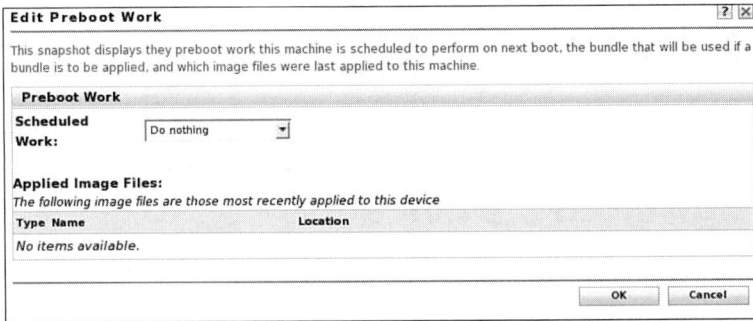

**Edit Preboot Work**

This snapshot displays they preboot work this machine is scheduled to perform on next boot, the bundle that will be used if a bundle is to be applied, and which image files were last applied to this machine.

**Preboot Work**

**Scheduled Work:** | Do nothing ▾ |

**Applied Image Files:**
*The following image files are those most recently applied to this device*

| Type Name | Location |
|---|---|
| *No items available.* | |

OK    Cancel

6. Choose the desired value in the scheduled work: Do Nothing, Apply Preboot Bundle, Take an Image.

   ■ Apply Preboot Bundle displays the screen shown in Figure 7.21. From these fields you can select a bundle from the drop-down list. This holds a list of all the bundles that are assigned or indirectly assigned to the device. If no bundle is defined you may press the Browse button and select a preboot bundle. This causes the selected bundle to be assigned to the device. The other fields display information about the selected preboot bundle.

**FIGURE 7.21**
Sample Apply Preboot Bundle option on the Preboot Work Advanced page.

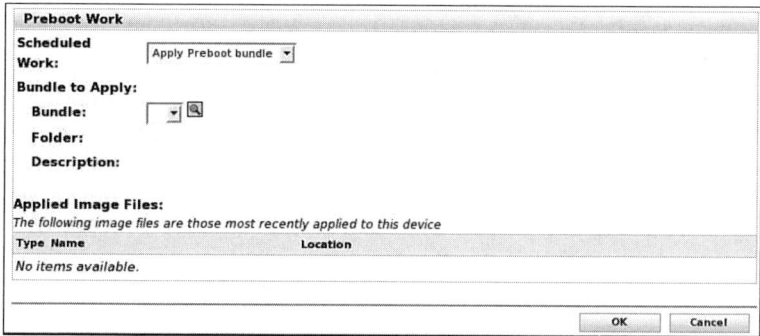

- Selecting Take Image displays Figure 7.22. This option requires that you enter the path and name of the image file to create when taking an image of the device. Additionally, you can select the level of compression for the image file.

**FIGURE 7.22**
Sample Take Image option on Preboot Work page.

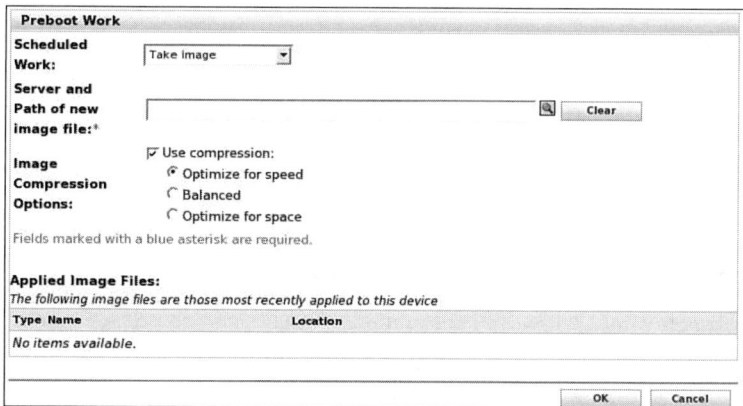

7. Press OK. The next time the device boots, the system applies the selected preboot bundle.

# Updating Previously Created Bundles

Sometimes you want to update previously created bundles. This can be to add RPMs, delete RPMs, or modify their entries. Whenever any change is made to a bundle, ZENworks automatically creates a new version for the bundle.

When there are multiple versions of a bundle, you have the option of selecting which bundle you want to be the delivered bundle to assigned devices. When the device verifies that all assigned bundles have been assigned, the device recognizes when a previously delivered bundle has a new version number. If the version number is different than the previously applied bundle, the newly selected bundle is applied to the device.

To select the version of a bundle, follow these steps:

1. Launch the ZENworks Control Center.
2. Browse to and select the desired bundle.
3. Click on the Details tab of the bundle.
4. Press the drop-down list next to the version label. Select the desired version. Click on the Deploy button to mark the selected version as the version of the bundle to deploy to assigned devices.

# Bundle Groups

To simplify the management of a set of bundles, ZENworks enables you to create a bundle group. A bundle group constitutes a set of defined bundles. You can then assign the set of bundles with a single action by assigning the bundle group.

When a bundle group is assigned to a device, all the bundles represented in the group are installed on the device.

Create a bundle group by doing the following tasks:

1. Launch ZENworks Control Center.
2. Select the Bundles tab at the top of the screen.
3. Browse to the folder within the bundles where you want to create the bundle group.
4. Click on the New menu option and select Bundle Group. Figure 7.23 shows a sample first screen of the wizard. Press Next.

**FIGURE 7.23**
Representative first page of Create Bundle Group wizard.

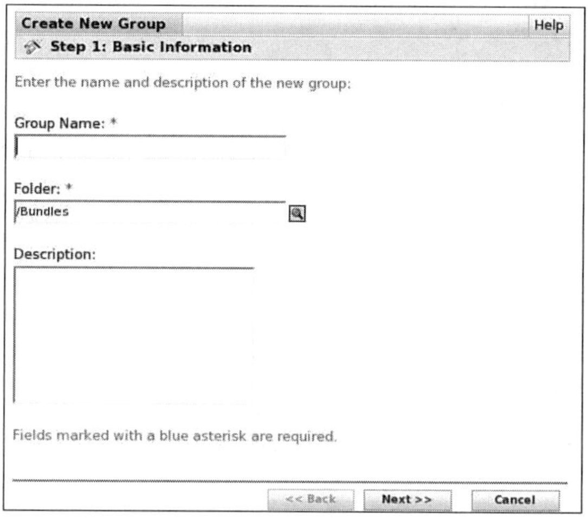

**5.** This displays the summary screen. This only creates the bundle group, but it has no bundles as members. You can assign bundles into the group at a later time or you can do it now by pressing the Next button. The Add wizard page is displayed (see Figure 7.24).

**FIGURE 7.24**
Sample Add Members page of Group Wizard.

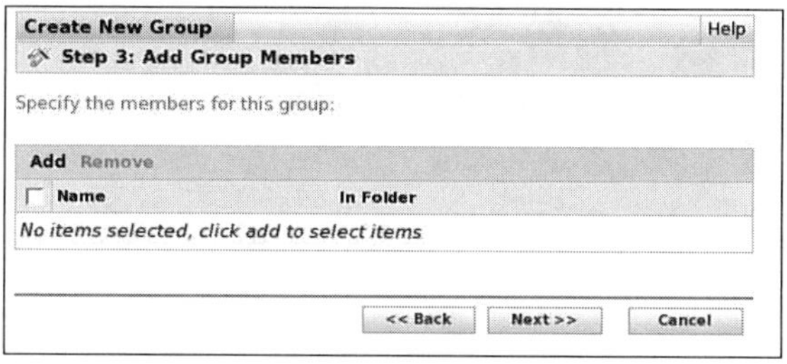

**6.** On the Add page, click on the Add button and browse to and select one or more bundles you want to add to this group. Press OK on the pop-up dialog to return to this page. Press Next.

**7.** The next page enables you to assign this group to any devices, groups, or folders. If you want to assign the group at this time, press the Add button. Then select the desired devices and press OK to exit the pop-up dialog box. Press Next.

8. The next screen is the summary screen. Press Finish to complete the bundle group creation.

You have now successfully created a bundle group. You can modify the bundle group by selecting the group and then using the snapshots displayed on the Add or Remove Members screen.

# Conclusion

This chapter discussed the creation and assignment of bundles and bundle groups. Bundles contain sets of RPM files or references to image files on ZENworks servers. RPM bundles assigned to a device cause that device to install those packages. Assigning a preboot bundle assigns a specific image to the device so when a re-image is requested, that image is applied.

Users of previous versions of ZENworks Linux Management will see that packages are now placed into bundles that can be assigned. Also, you will see later that catalogs are much like channels in previous versions of ZENworks Linux Management. The enhancement with ZENworks 7 is that bundles perform the installation without requiring a transaction to identify specific RPMs.

Those of you who have a background in the traditional ZENworks product will recognize that bundles are much like Application Objects from ZENworks Desktop Management and Distributions from ZENworks Server Management. Bundles represent content to be delivered to any device.

# CHAPTER 8

# Catalogs

This chapter discusses catalogs in the ZENworks 7 Linux Management product. Catalog creation, modifications, and assignments, like all administrative functions, are performed in the ZENworks Control Center.

## What Are Catalogs?

A catalog goes hand in hand with RPM bundles and is simply an ordered collection of RPM bundles. (See Chapter 7, "Bundles.") Catalogs can be assigned and delivered to a managed device.

Although RPM bundles are stored in the ZENworks Linux Management database, catalogs are objects that are stored in the ZENworks Object Store. See Chapter 13, "ZENworks Linux Management Database," for more information.

## What Are the Advantages of Catalogs?

Catalogs are used for dependency resolution, as well as to install optional software. Dependency resolution occurs when an RPM bundle has requirements that are not already met or when dependent RPMs in the catalog are automatically installed.

## How to Create a Catalog

Complete the following steps to create a catalog in ZENworks 7 Linux Management:

1. Launch a browser and enter the URL of the ZENworks Control Center.

2. Log in to the ZENworks Control Center.

3. Click Bundles on the menu tab at the top of the page.

4. Click the New drop-down menu and choose Catalog. This starts the Catalog Creation Wizard (see Figure 8.1).

**FIGURE 8.1**
Step 1 of the Catalog Creation Wizard.

Bundles > Create New Catalog

Create New Catalog

Step 1: Catalog Name

Specify the name, description, and display name for the new catalog:

Catalog Name: *

Display Name: *

Folder: *
/Bundles

Description:

Fields marked with a blue asterisk are required.

<< Back    Next >>    Cancel

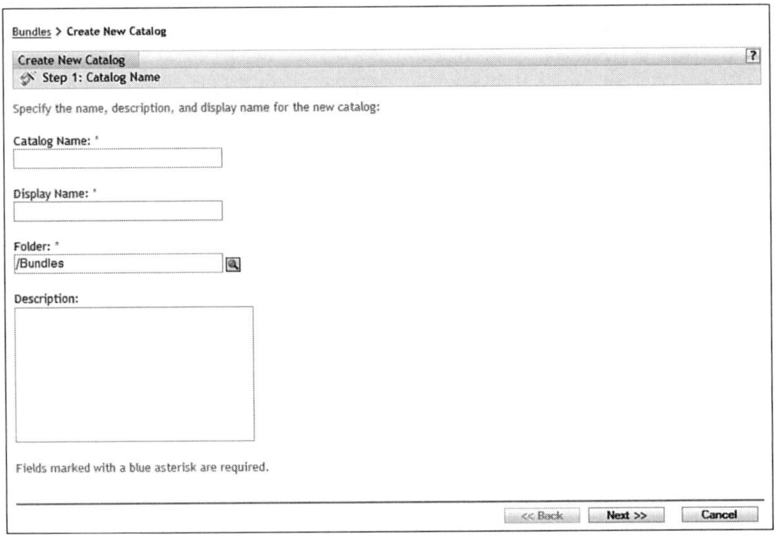

Complete the wizard to create a catalog. The steps of the wizard are described in the following sections.

# Catalog Creation Wizard: Catalog Name

During step 1 of the wizard you must enter the following information:

- **Name**—Enter the catalog's name. This is the name that will be displayed in the ZENworks Control Center for this catalog.

- **Display Name**—Enter the name of the catalog that should be displayed on the end-user interface system.

- **Folder**—Browse to the folder under the Bundles area where you want this catalog to be created. Folders help you organize your catalogs.

- **Description**—Enter a text description if you desire. This description is used to assist you in remembering what this catalog may contain.

Press Next. This advances the wizard to step 2, where you specify the Catalog Attributes.

## Catalog Creation Wizard: Catalog Attributes

Step 2 displays a screen similar to Figure 8.2.

**FIGURE 8.2**
Step 2 of the Catalog Creation Wizard, to assign attributes.

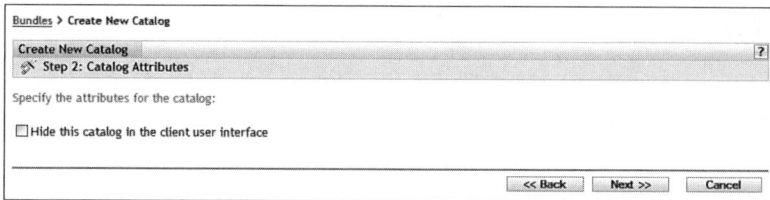

On step 2 of the wizard you are simply asked whether you want to hide the catalog from the user on the client machine.

Hiding a catalog is a good idea if you are using it to deploy software that has dependent RPM packages. This way you don't have to rely on the user installing software. For example, you would hide a catalog that is used to deploy virus patterns that are dependent upon the antivirus software being installed.

To hide a catalog, mark the check box next to Hide This Catalog in the Client User Interface.

## Catalog Creation Wizard: Summary

Step 3 of the wizard is the Summary page. The Summary page displays all aspects of the catalog. See Figure 8.3.

Review the summary page and press Back to return to a previous page to make changes, Cancel to terminate the catalog creation, or Finish to complete and create the catalog.

After you press the Finish button, the ZENworks Control Center displays the success in the catalog creation. Press OK to return to the ZENworks Control Center.

**FIGURE 8.3**
*The Summary page of the Catalog Creation Wizard.*

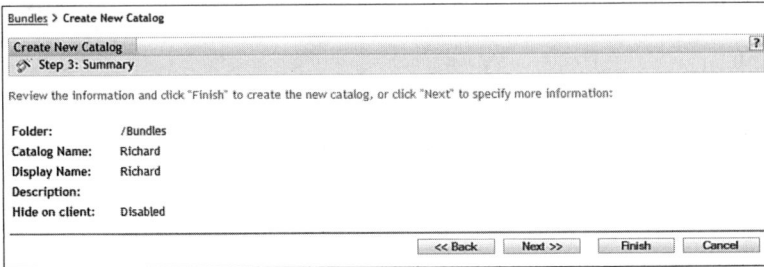

Bundles > Create New Catalog

Create New Catalog
Step 3: Summary

Review the information and click "Finish" to create the new catalog, or click "Next" to specify more information:

Folder:            /Bundles
Catalog Name:      Richard
Display Name:      Richard
Description:
Hide on client:    Disabled

<< Back    Next >>    Finish    Cancel

# Adding RPM Bundles to Catalogs

Catalogs do not do anything unless you add RPM bundles to them. There are a couple of different ways to do this. The easiest way to add an RPM bundle or bundles to a catalog is by doing the following:

1. Open the ZENworks Control Center.

2. Click on Bundles on the menu at the top of the screen.

3. Select the specific bundle or bundles by clicking on the check box in the list next to the bundles you want to add. This activates the rest of the Bundles menu.

4. Select the Action menu item to open the drop-down list and select Add to Catalog. This launches the Add to Catalog Wizard. See Figure 8.4.

**FIGURE 8.4**
The Add to Catalog Wizard.

Bundles > Add To Catalog

Add To Catalog
Step 1: Targets

Select the catalogs that will contain the items.

Add  Remove
☐ Name                              In Folder
No items selected, click add to select items

<< Back    Next >>    Cancel

5. Click the Add button on the menu and choose the catalogs you want to contain the RPM bundles. Then click Next.

6. Press Back to return to a previous page to make changes, Cancel to terminate the wizard, or Finish to complete the wizard.

# How to Assign a Catalog to a Device

When a catalog is assigned to a device, either directly or indirectly, ZENworks installs the RPM bundles in the catalog to that device.

A catalog that is newly assigned to a device is installed when the next bundle refresh cycle occurs. This can happen at boot time or based on the bundle refresh setting in the managed device's zone.

You can follow a couple of methods to assign a bundle to a device. One method is as follows:

1. Open the ZENworks Control Center.

2. Click on Devices on the menu at the top of the screen.

3. Browse within the Devices folder to the folder where the specific device is located.

4. Select the specific device by clicking on the check box in the list next to the device. This activates the rest of the Device menu.

5. Select the Action menu item to open the drop-down list and select Assign Catalog. This launches the Assign Catalog Wizard. See Figure 8.5.

**FIGURE 8.5**
The Assign Catalog Wizard.

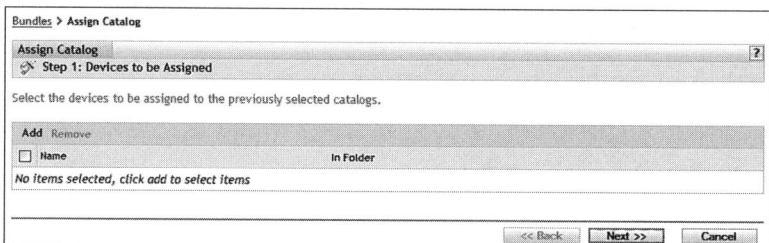

Bundles > Assign Catalog

**Assign Catalog**
Step 1: Devices to be Assigned

Select the devices to be assigned to the previously selected catalogs.

**Add** Remove

☐ Name        In Folder

*No items selected, click add to select items*

<< Back    Next >>    Cancel

6. Click Next to move to step 2 of the wizard to set Special Flags. See Figure 8.6.

**FIGURE 8.6**
Step 2 of the Assign Catalog Wizard, Special Flags.

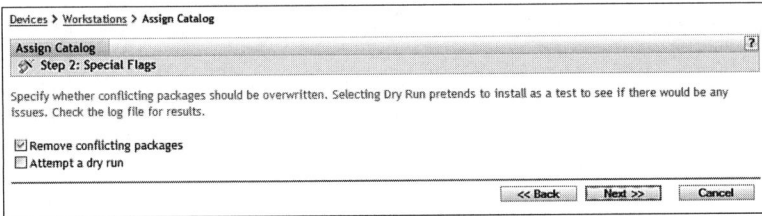

During this step you see two options:

- **Remove Conflicting Packages**—This option enables you to specify whether conflicting packages should be overwritten.

- **Attempt a Dry Run**—Checking this option simulates the installation to test to see whether there will be any issues or conflicts. The results of the dry run are stored in the log file.

7. Press Back to return to a previous page to make changes, press Cancel to terminate the wizard, or press the Finish button to complete the wizard.

Another method to assign a catalog is the following:

1. Open the ZENworks Control Center.

2. Click on Bundles on the menu at the top of the screen.

3. Select the specific catalog by clicking on the check box in the list next to the catalog you want to assign. This activates the rest of the Bundles menu.

4. Select the Action menu item to open the drop-down list and select Assign Catalog. This launches the Assign Catalog Wizard.

You can also assign a catalog by going directly to the device or device group.

# What Happens When a Catalog Is Assigned to a Device

When a catalog is assigned to a device, ZENworks attempts to install the RPM bundles in the order in which they are listed in the catalog. When the device performs a refresh, which is done at boot time or when the scheduled refresh interval is reached, the device becomes aware of any newly assigned catalogs.

To change the order of RPM Bundles in a catalog, follow these steps:

1. Open the ZENworks Control Center.
2. Click on Bundles on the menu at the top of the screen.
3. Click on the name of the catalog you want to modify. You see a screen similar to Figure 8.7.

**FIGURE 8.7**
The Catalog Summary page.

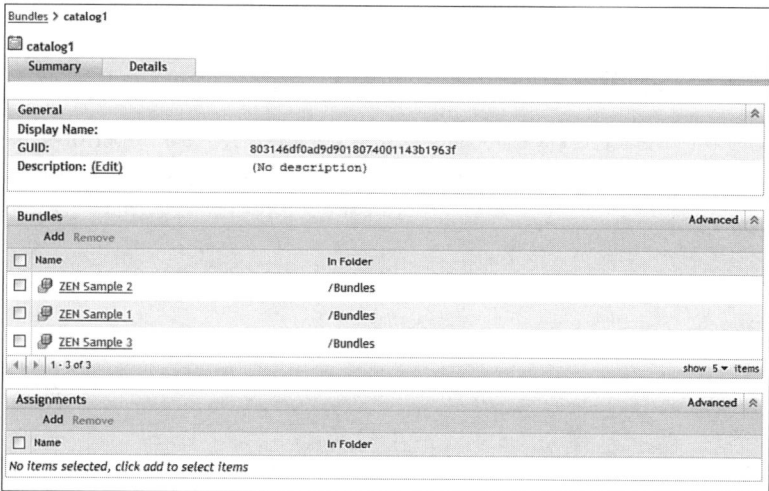

4. Click the Advanced option on the title bar of the Bundles snapshot. You see a screen similar to Figure 8.8.

**FIGURE 8.8**
The Edit Bundles Advanced page.

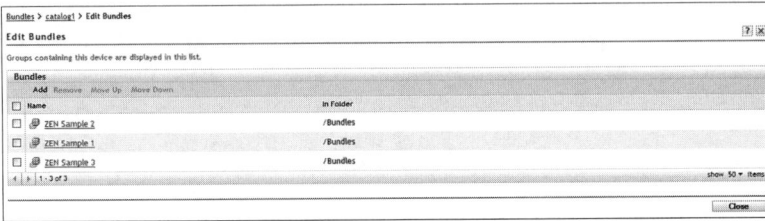

5. Check the boxes next to the bundles you want to move. This activates the rest of the menu options.

6. Choose either Move Up or Move Down to change the order of the selected bundle(s).

7. Click Close to go back to the Catalog Summary page.

# Conclusion

Catalogs provide a great way to deliver and install software and perform dependency resolution. They make it easier for you as the administrator and ensure that applications are installed and running properly.

# CHAPTER 9

# Policies

This chapter discusses policies in the ZENworks 7 Linux Management product. Policy creation, modifications, and assignments, like all administrative functions, are performed in the ZENworks Control Center.

## What Are Policies?

Policies are configurations that may be made to an operating system or application on a managed device. Security settings or default configurations, for example, can be set up in a policy.

After these policies are created, you can assign them to devices registered in your ZENworks system. When a device discovers (or is told) that it has a policy assigned, it retrieves the policy and applies that policy based on the schedule or event specified. When a policy is applied, the configurations are set on the operating system or application. Applying policies is the responsibility of enforcers that are installed on the device when the ZENworks 7 agent is installed.

## Why Are Policies Useful?

The reason that policies can be very powerful in managing your business environment is that you can create a single policy and, with just a click of the mouse, have that policy applied to hundreds and thousands of devices. After they are assigned, those devices automatically apply that policy. You can be confident that the policy is sent and enforced on the device.

Now if you decide to change a policy, simply edit it in ZENworks Control Center and the system automatically updates all assigned devices with that updated policy. You don't need to do a thing.

# How Are Policies Assigned?

Policies are assigned in the ZENworks Control Center through direct or indirect assignments. Regardless of whether a policy is assigned indirectly or directly, the policy is sent to the device and applied to the managed device.

## Direct Assignment

Directly assigned policies are policies that have been assigned directly to a managed device.

## Indirect Assignment

Indirectly assigned policies are policies that are effective for the device and have been assigned through a group membership or containment.

## Assigning a Policy

Several ways of assigning a policy to a device are available in the ZENworks Control Center. The following describes the different ways that you can assign a policy to a device:

- As part of the policy creation wizard.
- As an action in the standard ZENworks Control Center lists.
- During review of the details of a folder, policy, or device.
- In the command line on the managed device.

## Assigning a Policy with Creation Wizard

All policies are created through a policy creation wizard. Each wizard page is customized for the particular policy that is being created. Regardless of the type of policy created, all wizards present the same pages to allow for the assignment of the policy to managed devices, folders, or groups.

After the policy is defined in the wizard and you are viewing the summary page, you may either finish the policy definition by pressing the Finished button on the page or you may proceed in the wizard to select an assignment of the policy by pressing the Next button (see Figure 9.1).

**FIGURE 9.1**
Wizard page that allows policy assignments.

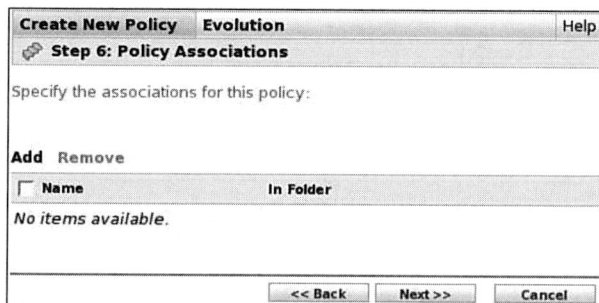

| Create New Policy | Evolution | | Help |
|---|---|---|---|
| | **Step 6: Policy Associations** | | |

Specify the associations for this policy:

**Add** Remove

| Name | In Folder |
|---|---|
| *No items available.* | |

<< Back    Next >>    Cancel

When you are viewing the Policy Assignment page, you can select devices, groups, or folders that are assigned the created policy. Complete the following steps to assign the policy:

1. Press the bold Add menu item in the middle of the screen.

2. The Select Assignments dialog box appears on the screen (see Figure 9.2).

**FIGURE 9.2**
The Select Associations pop-up dialog box.

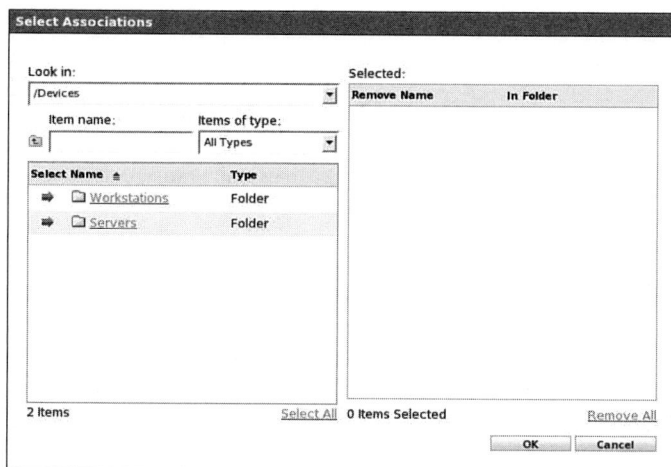

**Select Associations**

Look in:

/Devices

| Item name: | Items of type: |
|---|---|
| | All Types |

Selected:

| Remove Name | In Folder |
|---|---|

| Select Name ▲ | Type |
|---|---|
| ➡ Workstations | Folder |
| ➡ Servers | Folder |

2 Items     Select All    0 Items Selected     Remove All

OK    Cancel

**3.** Select the devices, groups, or folders to which you want to assign the policy. To drill into folders, select the green, underlined folder name. You can select the item by pressing the blue arrow to the left of the object name. When you select the item, it is displayed on the right pane of the dialog box (see Figure 9.3).

**FIGURE 9.3**
Selected items in the Select Associations pop-up dialog.

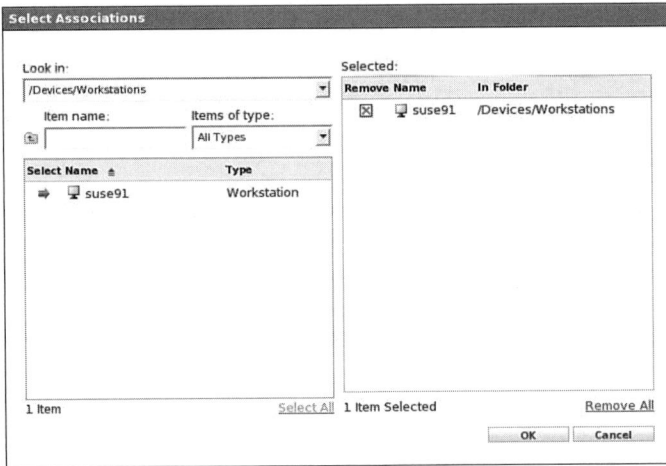

**4.** If you want to remove a selection that you have previously selected, click the red boxed X. This removes that item from the assignment list.

**5.** After you have completed your selections, press the OK button to make your assignments.

**6.** Complete the wizard by finishing the remaining pages.

# Assigning a Policy Through List View

While in the ZENworks Control Center and under the Devices folder you are presented with the Workstations and Servers folders. If you select either folder, the ZENworks Control Center drills into that folder and displays all the devices and subfolders. From any of these lists you may assign a policy to a device or folder.

Complete the following to assign a policy to a device in the ZENworks Control Center list view:

1. Select the Devices folder in the ZENworks Control Center (see Figure 9.4).

**FIGURE 9.4**
Devices folder in the ZENworks Control Center.

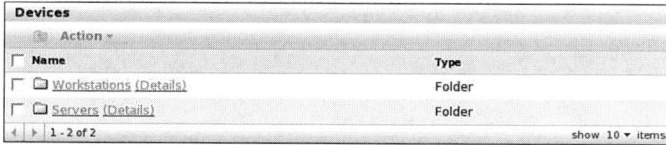

2. Select either the Workstations or Servers folder to drill into the folder and view any devices or subfolders (see Figure 9.5).

**FIGURE 9.5**
List view of the Workstations folder.

3. Select all the devices to which you want to assign the policy. Do so by selecting the selection box next to the device. When one or more devices are selected, the Action menu item is activated.

4. Select the Action menu item to bring up the pop-up menu list.

5. Select the Assign Policy menu item. This brings up the Assign Policy wizard.

6. The first page of the Assign Policy wizard displays the devices that are to be assigned (see Figure 9.6). From this wizard page you may add additional devices by selecting the Add menu. You can also remove devices on this wizard page by selecting the selection box next to the devices and

selecting the Remove menu item. Press Next when you are finished with the selected devices.

**FIGURE 9.6**
First page of the Assign Policy Wizard: Devices to Be Assigned

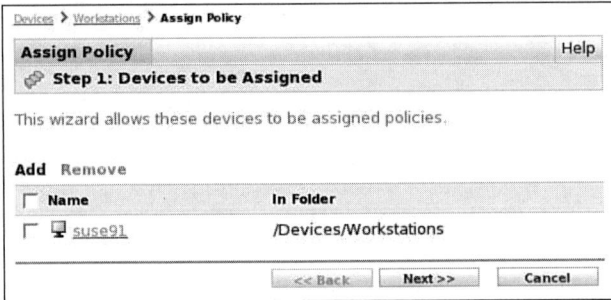

7. Step 2 of the Assign Policy Wizard enables you to select the policies that you want assigned to the selected devices in the previous step. Press the Add menu item and select the desired policies from the Select Objects dialog (see Figure 9.7).

**FIGURE 9.7**
Select Objects dialog.

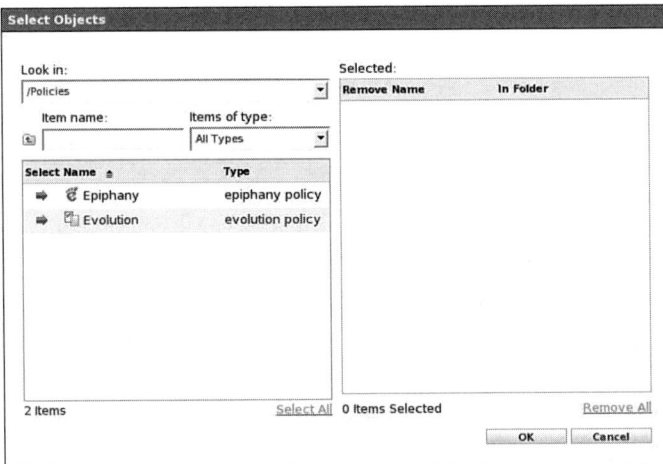

8. After you have selected the set of policies to assign, press OK in the Select Objects dialog.

9. The assigned policies are listed on the Step 2: Policies to Be Assigned page. From here you can continue to add policies or you can remove the policies from the list. Remove by selecting the selection box next to the policy and then pressing the Remove menu choice. After the list of policies is complete, press Next.

10. The next page of the Assign Policy Wizard enables you to select the schedule within which the policy will become effective. When the schedule occurs, the policy is placed on the workstation. If None is selected for the schedule type, the policy will never be enforced on the assigned devices. When you have completed the scheduling administration, press Next.

11. The summary page is displayed next, listing the policies and the devices, folders, or groups to which they have been assigned. Additionally, the page displays the schedule type and any details about the schedule. Press Finish to complete the wizard.

## Assigning a Policy in Folder Details

When you assign a policy to a folder, all the devices in that folder or any sub-folder are assigned the specified policy. To assign a policy to a folder, complete the following steps:

1. Browse to the listing that presents the desired folder. For example, Figure 9.8 shows the Devices folder, which contains two subfolders: Workstations and Servers.

**FIGURE 9.8**
Devices folder listing.

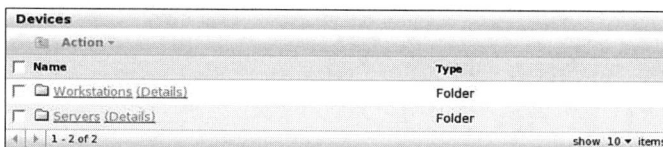

2. Press the check box next to the desired folder. This should cause the Action menu item to be activated.

3. Press the Action menu and choose Assign Policy from the pop-up menu.

**4.** This takes you through the Assign Policy Wizard, as described in the previous section.

You may also assign a policy to a folder by entering the folder's details. You enter a folder's details by pressing the Details link next to the folder name. Within that folder's details is an Effective Policies snapshot. You can use this method to assign policies in the same way as described in the following "Assigning a Policy in Policy Details" section.

When a policy is assigned to a folder, all devices in that folder and any subfolders receive that policy. This "inheritance" of a policy through a folder above can be overwritten by assigning a policy closer, in a hierarchical fashion, to the device.

For example, if PolicyA were assigned to Folder1, any devices in Folder1 and Folder1.1 would have PolicyA applied if they met the system requirements for that policy. If a separate PolicyA (called PolicyA1) were applied to Folder1.1, the devices in Folder1.1 would get PolicyA1 and would not get PolicyA. To discover which policies will be applied to a device, you can pretend to enter ZENworks at the location where the device is in the object store. Then walk up the folders searching for a policy. When you find a policy, you stop searching for that particular type of policy. You may continue to search up the folder hierarchy looking for other policies, but you will not apply any policy of the type that you had previously found.

The only exception to this rule is the Generic GNOME policy. This policy is cumulative, meaning that it is a merge of all the effective Generic GNOME policies that are associated to the device or a group or container of the device.

## Assigning a Policy in Policy Details

Within the ZENworks Control Center you can view the details of any policy. Within the details of the policy you can view or edit all the settings for the policy. Additionally, you can assign the policy to any device, group, or folder. Figure 9.9 shows a policy details page.

To assign the displayed policy, complete the following steps:

**1.** Scroll to the Associations snapshot on the page.

**2.** Press the Edit menu item on the Associations snapshot. This opens the snapshot into full-screen mode and allows editing of the Associations list (see Figure 9.10).

**FIGURE 9.9**
Details page for a policy.

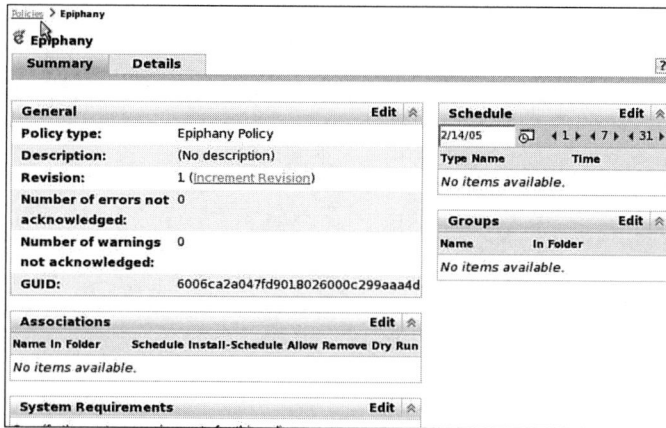

**FIGURE 9.10**
Associations list in Edit mode.

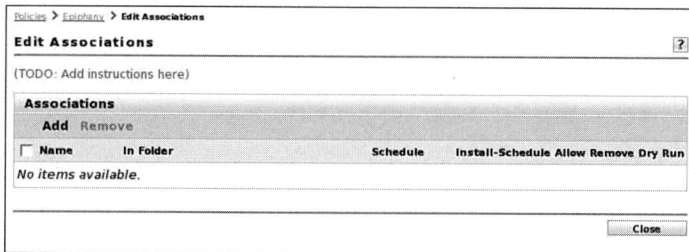

3. To add additional devices, groups, or folders to be assigned the policy, press the Add button. This brings up the Assign Policy Wizard as described earlier in the "Assigning a Policy Through List View" section.

4. When the addition is completed, press the Close button.

5. To remove assignments, select the devices, groups, or folders from the list by checking the check box next to the item. This should activate the Remove menu item.

6. Press the Remove menu item to remove the assignment.

7. Press the Close button when finished.

# Assigning a Policy in Device Details

Within the ZENworks Control Center you can view the details of any device. Within the details of the device you can view or edit all its settings. Additionally, you can assign any policy to the device.

To assign a policy to the displayed device, complete the following steps:

1. Locate the Effective Policies snapshot on the page. Figure 9.11 shows an example of this snapshot.

**FIGURE 9.11**
Effective Policies snapshot on a device details page.

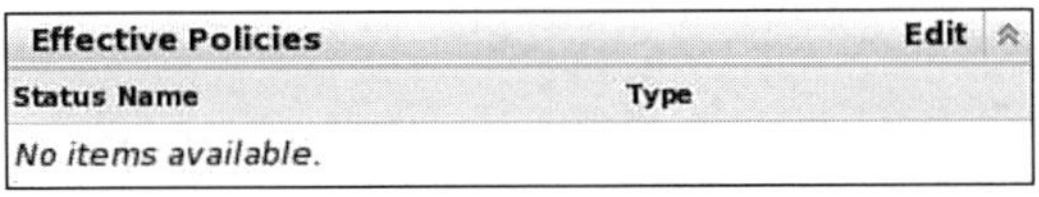

2. Press the Edit menu item on the snapshot. This opens the snapshot in full-page mode. Figure 9.12 displays a sample of this page.

**FIGURE 9.12**
Effective Policies in full-page mode.

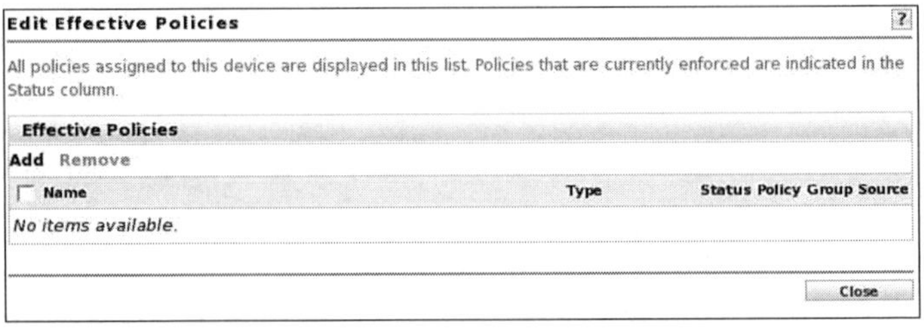

3. To assign a policy to this device, press the Add menu item. This brings up the Assign Policy Wizard as described earlier in the "Assigning a Policy Through List View" section.

4. When the addition is completed, press the Close button.

5. To remove assignments, select the policies from the list by checking the check box next to the item. This should activate the Remove menu item.

6. Press the Remove menu item to remove the assignment.

7. Press the Close button when finished.

## Assigning a Policy Through the Command Line

When ZENworks Linux Management is installed, an additional command-line tool is also installed on the primary and secondary servers. This tool is `zlman` and is located in the `/usr/bin` directory. This command-line tool enables you to perform almost any administrative function that can be done via the web browser interface.

To assign a policy using the command-line `zlman` tool, complete the following:

1. Log in to one of the ZENworks servers.

2. Use the following command:

   `Zlman workstation-add-policy <options> <workstation> <policy>`

3. Optionally add the following options:

   - `–user=<name>`, enter an administrator user name

   - `–password=<string>`, enter password for the user specified

Add additional options as desired. These can be found in Appendix A, "Commands."

# Policy Groups

ZENworks 7 Linux Management makes it possible to create policy groups. A policy group constitutes a set of policies that can be assigned via a single group. In all the places in ZENworks Control Center where a policy can be assigned, a policy group may be used. When a policy group is assigned to a device, group, or folder, the action effectively assigns all policies in that policy group.

To create a policy group, complete the following tasks:

1. Go to a Policies subfolder.

2. Select the Add menu item in the list view.

3. Select the Policy Group menu item from the pop-up menu. This starts up the Create New Group Wizard.

4. Enter a unique group name into the Group Name field. See Figure 9.13 for a sample screen.

**FIGURE 9.13**
Sample policy group creation wizard screen.

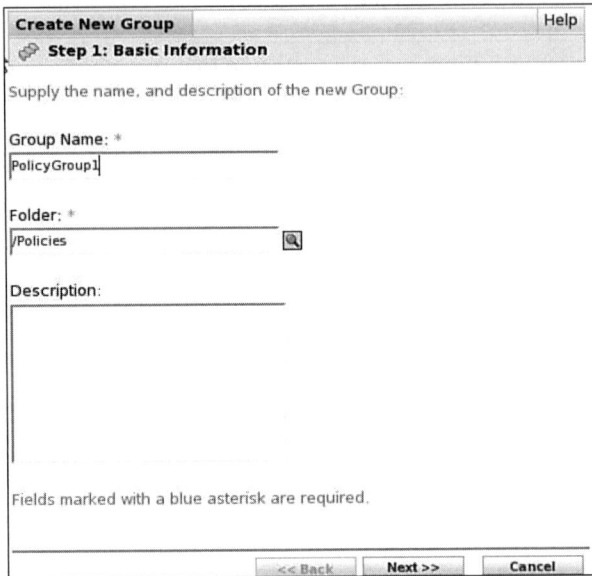

5. Browse and select the folder or subfolder where you would like the policy group to reside. The policy group may be assigned to any device, group, or folder, regardless of where it is stored in the ZENworks Control Center.

6. Enter any description you wish for the policy group. Press Next.

7. Press Next on the summary page to place policies into this newly created policy group.

8. The next screen displays the Add Group Members page, where you can browse to and select the policies you want to add to the group. See Figure 9.14 for a sample of this screen.

9. Press the Add menu item and browse to and select the policies you want to add to this policy group.

10. Remove any policies that you do not want to have in the group by selecting the check box next to the policy you want to remove. This should activate the Remove menu button.

11. Press the Remove button to remove the selected policies from the group. Press Next.

**FIGURE 9.14**
Sample Add Group Members page of the policy group creation wizard.

| Create New Group | Help |
|---|---|
| 🔗 Step 3: Add Group Members | |

Specify the members for this group:

**Add**  Remove

| ☐ Name | In Folder |
|---|---|
| *No items available.* | |

<< Back   Next >>   Cancel

12. On the next page you can actually assign this group to any device, folder, or group. Press Next when you have completed any assignments that you want. The summary page is displayed.

13. Review the summary page and press the Finished button to complete the policy group creation and membership assignments.

# Available Policies in ZENworks 7 Linux Management

Several policies have been created and defined in the ZENworks 7 Linux Management system. This section discusses each of the available policies.

## Epiphany Policy

Epiphany is a web browser provided as part of the GNOME desktop. ZENworks 7 Linux Management provides a policy that allows the configuration of an Epiphany browser on the assigned managed device.

Checking or unchecking the corresponding check box enables you to configure the following actions from the Epiphany policy. When a check box is selected, that action is activated.

- Disable JavaScript control of window chrome.
- Hide menu bar.
- Disable automatic downloading and opening of files.
- Disable manual URL entry.

- Disable bookmark editing.
- Disable toolbar editing.
- Disable history.
- Disable loading of content from unsafe protocols. Default safe protocols are HTTP and HTTPS.
- Add protocol to the Safe Protocol list.

The following options of the Epiphany browser policy have additional data entered. Additionally, beyond setting the values for the following options, the policy may lock the value. To lock the value, select the lock button next to the corresponding value. This prevents the user from modifying that value on the assigned managed device.

- **Home page URL**—Specify the default URL home page for the browser. No default home page URL is specified.
- **Download Folder**—Specify the local folder where the browser should place any downloaded files. No default folder is specified.
- **Allow Popups**—Specify whether pop-ups should be allowed. The default is Yes.
- **Allow Java**—Specify whether the execution of Java applications in the browser page should be allowed. The default is Yes.
- **Allow JavaScript**—Specify whether JavaScript on the page should be executed. The default is Yes.
- **Cookies**—Specify whether the cookies' acceptance should be set to Always Accept, Only from Sites You Visit, or Never Accept. The default is Always Accept.
- **Disk Space for Temporary Files**—Specify the amount of space, in megabytes, that should be reserved for temporary files. The default is 50MB.

# Evolution Policy

Evolution is an email, calendaring, and collaboration tool that is available from Novell, Inc. (See http://www.novell.com/products/desktop/features/evolution.html.)

Novell Evolution embraces mail, calendar, and address book standards to ease data sharing. Supported mail protocols include IMAP, POP, SMTP, and Authenticated SMTP, as well as Microsoft Exchange 2000 and 2003 and Novell

GroupWise. iCalendar support enables users in disparate collaboration servers to share meeting information, publish this information, and subscribe to calendars published on the Web (webcal). Lightweight Directory Access Protocol (LDAP) support enables users to access their existing company address books. Users can also share contact information by using vCard message attachments.

ZENworks provides a policy that enables administrators to configure Evolution clients on the managed devices. Configure settings by checking or unchecking the corresponding check box next to the setting. When a check box is selected, that component is activated and the user is unable to change that option. The following is a list of configurable settings of the Evolution policy:

- Apply filters to new messages options
- Secure Socket Layer (SSL) option
- Email signature
- Email server authentication method
- Automatically check for new mail option
- Send and draft mail folder locations
- Save password option
- Receive mail configuration
- Send mail configuration
- Show only subscribed folders (for IMAP Mail Accounts)
- Override server-supplied folder namespace (for IMAP Mail Accounts)

The following options of the Evolution policy have additional data entered. Additionally, beyond placing the default values for the following options, the policy may lock the value. Lock the value by selecting the lock button next to the corresponding value. This prevents the user from modifying that value on the assigned managed device.

- **Default Character Encoding for Display**—The default value is Western European (ISO-8859-1). Choose the drop-down list to select any of the other 25 language values.

- **Default Character Encoding for Composed Mail**—The default value is Western European (ISO-8859-1). Choose the drop-down list to select any of the other 25 language values.

- **Empty Trash Folders on Exit**—The default value is Never; however, the optional values include Every Time, Once per Day, Once per Week, or Once per Month.

- **Check Inbox for Junk Mail**—The default value is Yes.

- **Include Remote Junk Mail Tests**—The default value is Yes.

- **Loading Images**—The default value for this field is Never Load Images off the Net. Optional values include Load Images if Sender Is in Address Book, or Always Load Images off the Net.

- **Mime Types Available for Viewing Attachments**—By default there are no mime types selected. The optional mime types that can be put into the available list include such items as PDF, GPG, PostScript, RTF, and 234 additional mime types. Select the mime types that you want to allow from the available list and then click the arrow buttons to move the selected items into and out of the selected list.

# Firefox Policy

Firefox is a streamlined web browser provided by Mozilla. ZENworks Linux Management provides a policy that enables you to configure and lock down the Firefox browser on any of the managed devices.

You can configure the following options for the Firefox policy by checking or unchecking the corresponding check box. When a check box is selected, that component is activated.

- Disable JavaScript control of window chrome

- Disable URL bar

- Disable bookmark editing

- Disable toolbar editing

- Disable history

- Disable saving of passwords

- Disable updates to themes

- Disable updates to extensions

The following options of the Firefox policy have additional data entered. Additionally, beyond placing the default values for the following options, the policy may lock the value. To lock the value, select the lock button next to the corresponding value. This prevents the user from modifying that value on the assigned managed device.

- **Homepage URL**—The default value is not initially defined. You need to enter the default value into the Homepage field.
- **Allow Popups**—The default value is Yes.
- **Allow Java**—The default value is Yes.
- **Allow JavaScript**—The default value is Yes.
- **Allow Sites to Set Cookies**—The default value for this setting is Yes. There is then an additional value that complements this setting: Keep Cookies. The Keep Cookies value defaults to Until They Expire. Optional values for this setting include Ask Me Every Time, or Until I Close Firefox.
- **Allow Loading of Images**—The default value for this setting is Anywhere. Optional values include From Originating Website Only, or Never.
- **Disk Space for Temporary Files**—The default value for this field is set at 50MB.

## Generic GNOME Policy

The Generic GNOME policy is unlike any of the other policies that are available in ZENworks Linux Management. This policy allows the free selecting and setting of any Gconf configuration setting. These settings are used by operating systems and many applications. Providing this generic policy enables administrations to manage keys within the system.

There are two ways to create the GNOME policy: importing settings from an existing managed desktop or manually. The first page of the wizard asks you which you would prefer.

Should you choose to have ZENworks automatically retrieve effective settings from a managed device, the following steps will be taken:

- On the next page of the wizard you are asked to either select a device from the ZENworks system (because the device had been previously registered with the system) or enter a DNS name or IP address for a workstation to which you want to connect. Additionally you must also enter the user that represents the effective settings you want to collect. Press Next.

The collected keys are displayed on the next wizard page. If you chose to not collect keys from a device, an empty Gconf tree is displayed. Complete the following to edit the directories, keys, and values:

- To add a key or a directory, press the Add menu item and choose either Directory or Key. Enter the Directory or Key name and then for the key, the corresponding value.

- To remove a key, select a set of keys or directories from the list and press the Delete menu item. Deleted directories remove all keys in that directory and subdirectories.

- To edit a key, select the key and a pop-up dialog is presented where you can modify the key name and/or value.

## Novell Linux Desktop Policy

The Novell Linux Desktop policy enables you to configure a Novell Linux Desktop workstation.

You can configure the following options for the Novell Linux Desktop policy by checking or unchecking the corresponding check box. When a check box is selected, that component is activated.

- Disable launching of command line programs.
- Disable screen locking.
- Disable logging off.
- Disable panel configuration.
- Disable printing.
- Disable print setup.
- Disable applets. This setting also includes the set of applets that are available on the desktop. You can select any of the set of applets and press the arrow buttons to move or remove the applets from the Applets to Be Disabled box. The list of available applets includes Dictionary, Clock, Fish, Weather, OpenOffice Quickstart, Sticky Notes, Stock Update, Geyes, CD Player, Volume Control, and Address Book.

The following options of the Novell Linux Desktop policy have additional data entered. Additionally, beyond setting the default values for the following options, the policy may lock the value. Lock the value by selecting the lock button next to the corresponding value. This prevents the user from modifying that value on the assigned managed device.

- **Background image file name**—There is no default filename specified. You must specify a file local to the managed device (for example, `/opt/gnome/share/images/roses.jpeg`).

- **Background position**—The default setting is Centered. The optional values include Fill Screen, Scaled, Tiled, No Background.

- **Background shade**—The default value is Solid. The optional values include Vertical or Horizontal.

- **Theme file name**—There is no default filename specified for this value. You must specify a local theme file for the managed device (for example, `/opt/gnome/share/themes/small.gtk`).

- **Proxy settings**—This setting enables you to choose one of the following options:

    - Direct Internet connection.

    - Manual proxy configuration—Under this setting you may specify the following parameters: HTTP Proxy Address and Port, HTTP Secure Proxy and Port, FTP Proxy Address and Port, and Socks Proxy and Port.

    - Automatic proxy configuration with a specified Autoconfiguration URL.

## Remote Execute Policy

The Remote Execute policy enables you to specify when a script should be executed on the assigned managed device.

Execute the following to construct a Remote Execute policy:

1. After you specify the name and folder for the policy and any optional description, press Next.

2. Specify the executable type for this policy. Values include Script, Binary, or Java.

3. Specify the maximum wait time for the execution to complete. You may choose from any of three choices:

    - Do not wait.

    - Wait until the program completes the execution.

    - Wait for X seconds. You may enter the number of seconds for ZENworks to wait for the execution to complete.

If you chose to run a script, follow these steps:

1. Specify the script to run. Your choices include Specify a File or Define Your Own Script. If you choose to specify a file, enter the path to the

script file in the Script File Name field. The script must already be on the managed device. If you choose to define your own script, a box appears in the screen and you can enter the script manually into the box.

2. Specify the additional parameters for the script: Script Parameters, Script Engine, and Script Engine Parameters. When the script is to be executed, ZENworks launches the specified script engine to run the script, with the parameters specified. Press Next.

If you chose to run a Binary or Java file, follow these steps:

1. Specify the executable filename. The executable file must already exist on the managed device.

2. Specify any executable parameters you want to give to the executable file.

If you chose to run a Java file, follow these steps:

1. Enter the Java program name. The Java file must already exist on the managed device.

2. Enter any program parameters you want to send to the Java program when it is launched.

3. Enter the path to the JRE (Java Run-time Engine) that will be used to run the Java program. The JRE must already have been installed on the managed device.

4. Enter the JRE parameters you want included in the launching of the program.

Press Next to get a summary of the execution policy, and then Finish to have the policy created.

## Text File Policy

The Text File policy enables the administrator to modify any text files on the managed device.

Complete the following steps to create and define your Text File policy:

1. Complete the name and folder where you want to have the policy. Enter any additional description and press Next.

2. Enter the name of the file you want to modify.

3. Enter the maximum number of revisions you want to keep. The default value is 5. Whenever ZENworks begins to modify a text file, it saves a

backup copy of the file before proceeding. This parameter specifies the number of copies to keep.

4. Enter a change name. You may have a number of changes in the Text File policy. Each change must be given a name.

5. Choose the type of change: Search File, Append Lines to File, Prepend Lines to File.

If you choose the Search File type, complete the following:

1. Enter in a search string, using regular expression formats.

2. Mark whether the search should be case sensitive. The default is to be case sensitive.

3. Select the search occurrence option. This option may be any of the following: First Occurrence, Last Occurrence, or Find All Occurrences.

4. Select the resulting action after an occurrence is found. The options include the following:

   - Add Lines After the Current Line
   - Add Lines Before the Current Line
   - Add String After
   - Add String Before
   - Add Word After
   - Add Word Before
   - Append String to Line
   - Prepend String to Line
   - Delete String
   - Delete Line
   - Delete All Lines After
   - Delete All Lines Before
   - Replace String
   - Replace Line
   - Replace All Lines After
   - Replace All Lines Before
   - Append String to File if Not Found
   - Prepend String to File if Not Found

**5.** Enter the new string in the text box provided and press Next.

If you choose to append or prepend lines to the file, just enter the text you want placed into the file. Press Next.

The Text File Policy also enables you to specify that a script, binary file, or Java application should be executed before changes are made to the text file. This can be useful, for example, if you need to stop some daemon before its configuration file is modified. The additional administration involved in choosing Script or Binary or Java is the same as described earlier in the "Remote Execute Policy" section.

Execute the following to complete the policy:

**1.** After entering any execution that should be completed prior to changes, select how you want ZENworks to behave should the execution fail. The execution fails if it returns a non-zero value to ZENworks. The options include Continue Modifying the Text Files and Do Not Modify the Text Files.

**2.** Choose any executable you want to run after the text file editing has been completed. This is defined in the same manner as in the prior step. Press Next.

**3.** Complete the wizard and press Finish.

To add changes to the policy, you must browse to the policy and then select to see the details of that policy. There you may add changes to the one file or add files to change.

To add changes, select the file and select New, Change, and enter the changes requested. All the changes are entered into a dialog box that mimics the wizard.

To add another text file to change, select the New, File menu option and enter the filename. All the changes are entered into a dialog box that mimics the wizard.

# Conclusion

Any editing to policies may be completed by browsing to the policy and selecting the details of the policy.

Policies can be very powerful tools that enable you to manage many devices by simply creating the policy and assigning it to as many devices as you choose. The system automatically applies the assigned policies to that managed device.

All assignments of policies are reflected in the Effective Policies snapshot that is present on all devices. Additionally, messages are sent from the devices to the ZENworks server to record whether and when policies are applied to the managed devices.

# CHAPTER 10

# Reporting

This chapter discusses reporting in the ZENworks 7 Linux Management product. Reporting, like all administrative functions, is performed in the ZENworks Control Center.

Through the reporting features of ZENworks Linux Management, you may create, delete, modify, and generate reports. The output from the reports may be printed or exported to HTML, XML, or a CSV file.

Reports in ZENworks Linux Management enable you to create tabular formatted output using inventory data (both hardware and software) that has been collected from the managed devices in the network.

## Creating Reports

You can create a report in ZENwork 7 Linux Management by executing the following steps:

1. Open your browser and enter the URL for the ZENworks Linux Management primary server (for example, http://server/zenworks).

2. Log in with your administrator account by entering your admin account and password. Press Login.

3. Click on the Reports menu at the top of the toolbar on the page. You should see a display similar to Figure 10.1.

**FIGURE 10.1**

Initial Reports home page in the ZENworks Control Center.

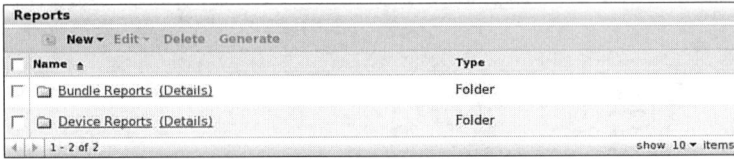

| Reports | |
|---|---|
| New ▾ Edit ▾  Delete  Generate | |
| ☐ **Name** ▴ | **Type** |
| ☐ 🗀 Bundle Reports (Details) | Folder |
| ☐ 🗀 Device Reports (Details) | Folder |
| ◂ ▸ 1 - 2 of 2 | show 10 ▾ items |

4. Click on the New menu selection and choose Report from the drop-down list. This starts the Create a New Report Wizard, which walks you through the creation of a report. Step 1 of the wizard should be similar to Figure 10.2.

**FIGURE 10.2**

Step 1 (Report Information) of the Create a New Report Wizard.

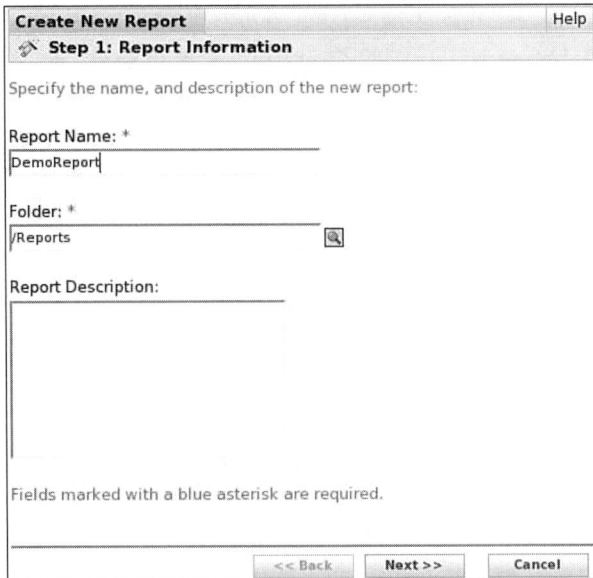

**Create New Report**                                    Help

**Step 1: Report Information**

Specify the name, and description of the new report:

Report Name: *

DemoReport

Folder: *

/Reports                                   🔍

Report Description:

Fields marked with a blue asterisk are required.

<< Back      Next >>      Cancel

5. Browse to and select any folders under the Reports category where you want this report definition to reside. By default all reports are under the root /Reports folder.

6. Enter a report name into the Report Name field.

**7.** Optionally enter a report description into the supplied text box. Press Next. Step 2 of the wizard should be similar to Figure 10.3.

**FIGURE 10.3**
Step 2 (Columns) of the Create a New Report Wizard.

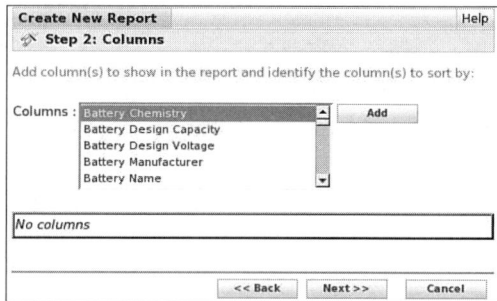

**8.** In Step 2 of the report wizard you define the columns that you want in your report. Don't worry about getting everything right at this point; you can always edit this aspect after the report is created. Begin by pressing the drop-down arrow on the Columns field to select the data you want reported. The name of the column is the name of the data member that you select.

The available data members are listed in Table 10.1.

**TABLE 10.1**
Report and Filtering Data Members, Expressions, and Value Types

| DATA MEMBER | OPERATOR | VALUES |
| --- | --- | --- |
| Battery Chemistry | Has, Doesn't have | Lithium-ion, Nickel Metal Hydride, Nickel Cadmium, Lead Acid, Unknown, Lithium Polymer, Zinc air |
| Battery Design Capacity | <, >, =, >=, <=,<> | Numerical |
| Battery Design Voltage | <, >, =, >=, <=,<> | Numerical |
| Battery Manufacturer | Equal to, Contains | String |
| Battery Name | Equal to, Contains | String |
| Battery Serial Number | Equal to, Contains | String |
| Bios Manufacturer | Equal to, Contains | String |
| Bios Name | Equal to, Contains | String |
| Bios Primary | <, >, =, >=, <=,<> | Numerical |

**TABLE 10.1**
Report and Filtering Data Members, Expressions, and Value Types (Continued)

| DATA MEMBER | OPERATOR | VALUES |
| --- | --- | --- |
| Bios Release Date | Before, After, Relative | Date and Time or Hours ago |
| Bios SMBios Version | Equal to, Contains | String |
| Bios Size (bytes) | <, >, =, >=, <=,<> | Numerical |
| Bios Version | Equal to, Contains | String |
| Bundle Creation Date | Before, After, Relative | Date and Time or Hours ago |
| Bundle Description | Equal to, Contains | String |
| Bundle Display Name | Equal to, Contains | String |
| Bundle Explorable | Is True, Is False | |
| Bundle Hidden | Is True, Is False | |
| Bundle Latest | Is True, Is False | |
| Bundle Name | Equal to, Contains | String |
| Bundle Path | Equal to, Contains | String |
| Bundle Version | <, >, =, >=, <=,<> | Numerical |
| Bus Description | Equal to, Contains | String |
| CD Rom Description | Equal to, Contains | String |
| CD Rom Manufacturer | Equal to, Contains | String |
| Chassis Asset Tag | Equal to, Contains | String |
| Chassis Manufacturer | Equal to, Contains | String |
| Chassis Serial Number | Equal to, Contains | String |
| Chassis Type | Has, Doesn't Have | SubChassis, Expansion Chassis, Match System Chassis, Lunch Box, Space-Saving, Sub Notebook, All in One, Docking Station, Hand Held, Notebook, LapTop, Portable, Tower, Mini Tower, Pizza Box, Low Profile Desktop, Multi-system Chassis, Desktop, Sealed-Case PC, Unknown, Rack Mount Chassis, Other, Storage Chassis, Peripheral Chassis, Buss Expansion Chassis |

**TABLE 10.1**

Report and Filtering Data Members, Expressions, and Value Types (Continued)

| DATA MEMBER | OPERATOR | VALUES |
| --- | --- | --- |
| Chassis Version | Equal to, Contains | String |
| Device Alias | Equal to, Contains | String |
| Device Code Page | Equal to, Contains | String |
| Device GUID | Equal to, Contains | String |
| Device Hostname | Equal to, Contains | String |
| Device Inventory Scan Time | Before, After, Relative | Date and Time or Hours ago |
| Device Last Contact | Before, After, Relative | Date and Time or Hours ago |
| Device Port | <, >, =, >=, <=,<> | Numerical |
| Device Primary Address | Equal to, Contains | String |
| Device Registered Date | Before, After, Relative | Date and Time or Hours ago |
| Device Virtual Memory | Equal to, Contains | String |
| Device Visible Memory | Equal to, Contains | String |
| Floppy Disk Capacity (bytes) | <, >, =, >=, <=,<> | Numerical |
| Floppy Disk Description | Equal to, Contains | String |
| Keyboard Description | Equal to, Contains | String |
| Logical Disk Available Space (bytes) | <, >, =, >=, <=,<> | Numerical |
| Logical Disk File System Size (bytes) | <, >, =, >=, <=,<> | Numerical |
| Logical Disk File System Type | Equal to, Contains | String |
| Logical Disk Label | Equal to, Contains | String |
| Machine Asset | Equal to, Contains | String |
| Machine Model | Equal to, Contains | String |
| Machine Model Number | Equal to, Contains | String |
| Machine Serial # | Equal to, Contains | String |
| Machine Vendor | Equal to, Contains | String |
| Message | Equal to, Contains | String |
| Message Acknowledged | Before, After, Relative | Date and Time or Hours ago |

**TABLE 10.1**
Report and Filtering Data Members, Expressions, and Value Types (Continued)

| DATA MEMBER | OPERATOR | VALUES |
|---|---|---|
| Message Additional Information | Equal to, Contains | String |
| Message Cleared | Before, After, Relative | Date and Time or Hours ago |
| Message Component Name | Equal to, Contains | String |
| Message from This Type Object | Equal to, Contains | String |
| Message ID | Equal to, Contains | String |
| Message Logged Time | Before, After, Relative | Date and Time or Hours ago |
| Message Raised by UID | Equal to, Contains | String |
| Message Severity | Equal, Not Equal | Informational, Warning, Error |
| Message Type | Equal, Not Equal | Client, Server |
| Modem Manufacturer | Equal to, Contains | String |
| Modem Name | Equal to, Contains | String |
| Monitor Description | Equal to, Contains | String |
| Monitor Manufacture Date | Before, After, Relative | Date and Time or Hours ago |
| Monitor Manufacturer | Equal to, Contains | String |
| Monitor Model | Equal to, Contains | String |
| Monitor Serial Number | Equal to, Contains | String |
| Monitor Viewable Size | <, >, =, >=, <=,<> | Numerical |
| Motherboard Description | Equal to, Contains | String |
| Motherboard Manufacturer | Equal to, Contains | String |
| Motherboard Number of Slots | <, >, =, >=, <=,<> | Numerical |
| Motherboard Version | Equal to, Contains | String |
| Network Adapter MAC Address | Equal to, Contains | String |
| Network Adapter Manufacturer | Equal to, Contains | String |

**TABLE 10.1**

Report and Filtering Data Members, Expressions, and Value Types (Continued)

| DATA MEMBER | OPERATOR | VALUES |
|---|---|---|
| Network Adapter Maximum Speed (Mbps) | <, >, =, >=, <=,<> | Numerical |
| Network Adapter Name | Equal to, Contains | String |
| Network Adapter Slot | Equal to, Contains | String |
| Network Adapter Type | Equal to, Contains | String |
| Operating System Architecture | Equal to, Contains | String |
| Operating System Detected | Equal to, Contains | String |
| Operating System ID | <, >, =, >=, <=,<> | Numerical |
| Operating System Is Product Enabled | Is True, Is False | |
| Operating System Package Manager | Equal to, Contains | String |
| Operating System Primary Role | Equal to, Contains | String |
| Operating System Product Name | Equal to, Contains | String |
| Operating System Product Version | Equal to, Contains | String |
| Operating System Target Name | Equal to, Contains | String |
| Operating System Target Vendor | Equal to, Contains | String |
| Parallel Port Name | Equal to, Contains | String |
| Physical Disk Capacity (bytes) | <, >, =, >=, <=,<> | Numerical |
| Physical Disk Description | Equal to, Contains | String |
| Physical Disk Free Size (bytes) | <, >, =, >=, <=,<> | Numerical |
| Physical Disk Manufacturer | <, >, =, >=, <=,<> | Numerical |
| Physical Disk Number of Partitions | <, >, =, >=, <=,<> | Numerical |
| Physical Disk Removable | Has, Doesn't Have | |

**TABLE 10.1**

Report and Filtering Data Members, Expressions, and Value Types (Continued)

| DATA MEMBER | OPERATOR | VALUES |
|---|---|---|
| Physical Disk Serial Number | Equal to, Contains | String |
| Pointer Name | Equal to, Contains | String |
| Pointer Number of Buttons | <, >, =, >=, <=,<> | Numerical |
| Power Supply Description | Equal to, Contains | String |
| Processor Clock Speed (MHz) | <, >, =, >=, <=,<> | Numerical |
| Processor Description | Equal to, Contains | String |
| Processor Family Type | Has, Doesn't Have | AMD AthlonMP™ Processor Family, AMD AthlonXP™ Processor Family, Intel Xeon processor MP, K602+, AMD29000 Family, Itanium Processor, Pentium III, Pentium II Xeon, 6x86, Celeron, Pentium Processor with MMX Technology, Pentium Pro, Pentium Brand, Pentium 4 Processor, Pentium III Processor with Intel SpeedStep Technology, Pentium III Xeon, AMD Athlon Processor Family, K6-3, K6-2, K6 Family, K5 Family, AMD Duron Processor Family, Unknown, Other |
| Processor Maximum Speed (MHz) | <, >, =, >=, <=,<> | Numerical |
| Processor Name | Equal to, Contains | String |
| Processor Other Family Description | Equal to, Contains | String |
| Processor Role Description | Has, Doesn't Have | Video Processor, DSP Processor, Math Processor, Central Processor, Unknown, Other |

**TABLE 10.1**

Report and Filtering Data Members, Expressions, and Value Types (Continued)

| DATA MEMBER | OPERATOR | VALUES |
|---|---|---|
| Processor Upgrade Method | Has, Doesn't Have | Slot 2, Slot 1, LIF Socket, None, Replacement/Piggy Back, ZIF Socket, Slot M, Daughter Board, Unknown, Slot A, Other, 370 Pin Socket |
| RPM Architecture | Equal to, Contains | String |
| RPM Conflicts | Equal to, Contains | String |
| RPM Description | Equal to, Contains | String |
| RPM Epoch | $<, >, =, >=, <=, <>$ | Numerical |
| RPM Formal Name | Equal to, Contains | String |
| RPM Name | Equal to, Contains | String |
| RPM Obsoletes | Equal to, Contains | String |
| RPM Provides | Equal to, Contains | String |
| RPM Releases | Equal to, Contains | String |
| RPM Requires | Equal to, Contains | String |
| RPM Section | Equal to, Contains | String |
| RPM Summary | Equal to, Contains | String |
| RPM Version | Equal to, Contains | String |
| Serial Port Name | Equal to, Contains | String |
| Sound Adapter Description | Equal to, Contains | String |
| Sound Adapter Name | Equal to, Contains | String |
| Video Description | Equal to, Contains | String |
| Video Manufacturer | Equal to, Contains | String |
| Video Slot | Equal to, Contains | String |

9. Continue to create columns by selecting additional columns from the list and pressing the Add button. Figure 10.4 shows a sample of the screen to select columns for your report.

10. You can rearrange the columns by selecting the blue arrow above a column name. A left arrow moves that column one to the left, whereas a right arrow moves that column one to the right.

**FIGURE 10.4**
Step 2 (Columns) of the Create a New Report Wizard after a column is defined.

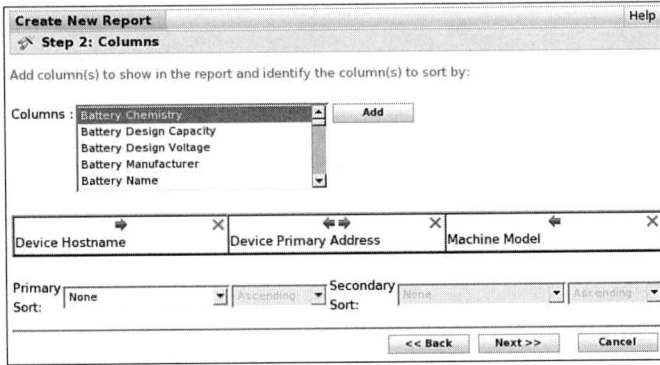

11. To remove a column, press the X in the top-right corner of the column you want to remove.

12. ZENworks Linux Management reporting also enables you to sort the report by specifying a primary and a secondary sort. If no sort is specified, the report is sorted automatically by the first column. Choose the primary sort by selecting the drop-down menu just to the right of the Primary Sort field. This displays a list of all of the columns in your report. Figure 10.5 shows a sample of selecting a filter for your report.

**FIGURE 10.5**
Step 2 (Columns) of the Create a New Report Wizard, selecting a sort.

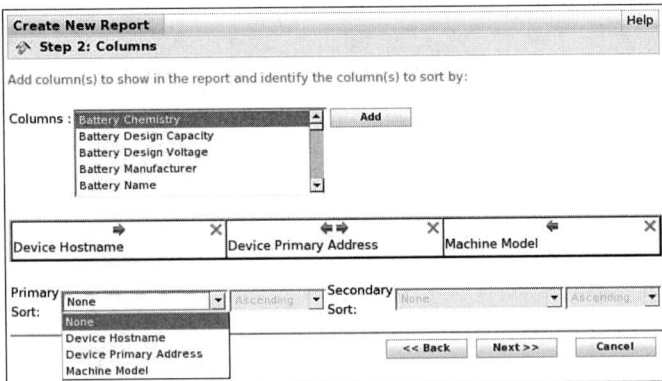

**13.** Next choose whether the sort should be ascending or descending based on the primary sort. Make the same selection for the secondary sort, if you choose. Press Next. Step 3 of the wizard should now be shown (see Figure 10.6).

**FIGURE 10.6**
Step 3 (Filters) of the Create a New Report Wizard.

**14.** On Step 3 of the wizard you may choose any filters that you want to limit the data that is selected from the system. If you chose not to do filtering, just press Next. If you want to filter the selections, complete the following:

  **a.** Select the New Filter menu item; this adds a filter line to the page.

  **b.** In the first field of the filter line, choose whether the filter should have a NOT.

  **c.** In the second field select one of any of the possible data members that are available in the system.

  **d.** In the third field you can select any Boolean or comparison operator that is appropriate for the member selected. Refer to Table 10.1 for a listing of these operators.

  **e.** If you want to remove a filter line, mark the check box next to the filter line and press the Remove menu item.

  **f.** As you add more filter lines, you will notice a small "or" is presented to the right. This helps you understand that the filter lines will be logically ORed together. For example, a two-filter line has the Boolean equivalent of saying "If filter1 or filter2 is true then include in the report."

  **g.** If you want to have the system perform a logical AND between filter lines rather than an OR, select the OR in the Sets Are to Be field. This causes all individual filters to be ANDed together and all groups (explained later) to be ORed together. So, for example, with a two-filter line and the Sets Are to Be field set to OR, the logic is "If filter1 and filter2 are both true for that record then include the item in the report."

h. For more complex filtering, you may construct groups of filters and have those groups ANDed or ORed together into a more complex Boolean expression. To add a group, press the New Sets menu item. When you do, all existing filters are considered to be in a group and a new group is presented on the page.

i. After you have constructed more than one filter set, changing the Sets Are to Be field causes a logical opposite effect to the full expression.

For example, if I have two filter sets, the first one saying "filter1 or filter2," and the second set saying "filter3 or filter4," and the Sets Are to Be field is set to AND, these sets will be ANDed together. This results in the following Boolean expression:

If (filter1 or filter2) and (filter3 or filter4) then include in report.

If you choose to have Sets Are to Be field set to OR, these sets are ORed together and the resulting Boolean logic is

If (filter1 and filter2) or (filter3 and filter4) then include in report.

You will notice that both the logic between the sets and the logic within the set flips to the opposite Boolean operator. This is necessary to keep the Boolean expression valid.

15. After you have completed your filter for the report, press Next.

16. The last page of the wizard gives a summary of your report. Press Back to return to the previous pages to make changes, or press Finish to complete the creation of the report.

17. The next screen shows a success or failure of the report creation.

18. Press OK. Now the new report you created appears in the report list.

# Running Reports

To run the previously defined or any of your created reports, go to the report folder that contains your desired report.

Select any of the reports you want to run. You may select the check box in the title bar to select all reports in the folder.

Press the Generate menu item and ZENworks runs each of the selected reports. When a report is completed, a browser window pops up with the report presented in the window.

You may also generate a report by pressing the Generate a Report quick task on the left task bar. This walks you through a wizard to generate any reports you select.

Figure 10.7 shows a sample report.

**FIGURE 10.7**
Sample generated report.

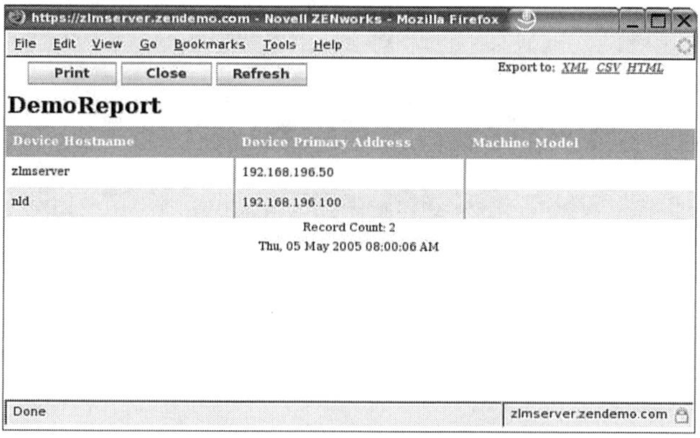

From the generated report you have several options presented in the button bar at the top left of the report. These buttons include

- **Print**—This sends the report to your printer.
- **Close**—This closes the report window.
- **Refresh**—This reruns the selected filtering options against the system and presents a newly run report in the same window.

# Saving Output of Reports

Often you want to take the output of a report and save it for later viewing. This can be done directly from the generated output of the report. Figure 10.7 shows a sample report.

On the right of the report are three hyperlink selections. These selections output the report in various formats to your hard drive. They include

- **XML**—This outputs the report in XML format suitable for parsing with execution code.
- **CSV**—This outputs the report in comma-separated format, suitable for importing into most databases, tables, or spreadsheets.
- **HTML**—This outputs the report in a browser format suitable for viewing in a browser.

After you select the type of output you want, the system prompts you for a filename and location. After those fields are completed, the system creates the local file and puts the output of the report in that file in the format specified.

# Editing an Existing Report

To edit an existing report, press on the hyperlink report name from the listing of reports on the screen (refer to Figure 10.1 for an example).

This shows you details of the report, including name, description, columns for the report, and any filtering. Modify any of the components you wish by completing the necessary actions as previously described in the wizard for that section.

# Conclusion

Reporting is a method for retrieving information out of the object store or the database. With ZENworks Linux Management and the ZENworks Control Center, you can define and generate all the reports you need.

# CHAPTER 11

# Common Device Management Tasks

This chapter discusses several of the common tasks that may be done in ZENworks Linux Management. Many of the tasks that you will want to perform can be found in the Quick Task area of the ZENworks Control Center.

## Viewing Getting Started

The first time that you launch and log in to the ZENworks Control Center you are presented with the Getting Started page. The Getting Started page gives you instructions, references, and links to other documentation to help you get ZENworks Linux Management working in your environment.

After you have entered into the ZENworks Control Center, the Getting Started page is not displayed on subsequent launches. If you wish to see the Getting Started page again, you need to go to the Home tab in the ZENworks Control Center and press the View Getting Started task in the Quick Task list.

## Managing Licenses

When ZENworks Linux Management is initially installed without a license code, the software is configured to be in evaluation mode. Evaluation mode is a fully functional product for 90 days from the installation. At the end of the 90 days, you can no longer manage the system through ZENworks Control Center.

When you have a license code, you can enter the code to fully license the ZENworks Linux Management product. This can be done by going to the Home tab on the ZENworks Control Center and then clicking on the Manage Licenses task in the Quick Task list.

Clicking on the Manage Licenses task brings up the Product Activation dialog, shown in Figure 11.1.

**FIGURE 11.1**
Product Activation dialog box.

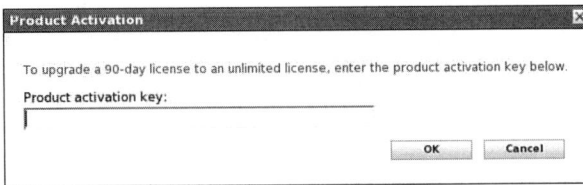

Enter the license code that was given at the time of purchase. When a valid code is entered, press the OK button.

# Clearing the Message Log

Messages are categorized as either Nn-Acknowledged, Acknowledged, or Cleared. When a message has not been acknowledged, it shows up on the status screens that show messages and events. When a message is acknowledged by the administrator action, the message is displayed only in the Advanced options of the event snapshot in the ZENworks Control Center.

On some occasions you may want to clear a message. When you clear a message, it still remains in the database, but is not displayed on the standard event snapshot and advanced options. Cleared messages can be displayed only via a report.

To clear the message log, do the following:

1. Launch ZENworks Control Center.

2. Log in as a ZENworks administrator.

3. Click on the Configuration tab.

4. Click on the Clear Message Log quick task. This displays a dialog to enable you to selectively clear the logs (see Figure 11.2).

**FIGURE 11.2**
Clear Message Log dialog.

5. Enter the beginning and ending dates that you want to clear.

6. Choose to clear the log by selecting the Clear radial button. If you want to permanently delete the selected logs, select the Permanently Delete radial button.

7. Press OK.

The logs are now cleared or deleted.

# Acknowledging All Events

When you are on a device's Details tab, there is an Acknowledge All Events task located in the quick task lists.

When you press the Acknowledge All Events task in the ZENworks Control Center, you mark all events against the specific device as being acknowledged. This does not remove the events from the message log, but does remove them from being shown on the events snapshot displayed for each device.

The messages that have been acknowledged may be viewed through the reporting features of ZENworks Linux Management.

# Controlling a Device Remotely

There are times when you may need to control a device remotely in the Zone. This can be done by launching the Remote Control task when you are in the devices list or on the details of a device. ZENworks Linux Management uses the open source VNC tool.

To control a device remotely, you must have the Java runtime installed on the managed device and the plug-in properly configured for the browser you are using. You can get the Java runtime and plug-in from www.java.com.

Additionally, for security, the remote control requires that the device have a password set. You can assign a password on the device by launching the following on the remote device:

```
/opt/novell/zenworks/sbin/zrmservice --passwd
```

This prompts you for a password to enter. This is normally run by a user to make sure that the password is known only by that user. The information is then passed to the help desk person to remote control the user's desktop. The user can clear the password by entering a --clrpasswd option.

When you select to control a device remotely, the ZENworks Control Center pops up the following dialog (see Figure 11.3).

**FIGURE 11.3**
Remote Management dialog.

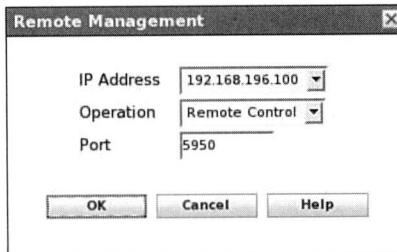

From the Remote Management dialog you can enter the following:

- **IP Address**—This is filled in automatically if the device is selected. If not, you need to enter the IP address of the device to be controlled.

- **Operation**—Choose the operation that you want to perform. The valid operations are Remote Control, Remote View, and Remote Login. If you choose Remote Control, the VNC agent is contacted on the device. If you choose Remote View, a remote control session is activated, but the administrator does not have control of the mouse or keyboard and therefore may only view the session. Lastly, if you choose to perform a Remote

Login, a new login session is started on the remote device and you are prompted for a username and password.

- **Port**—Enter the port that you have configured for VNC operations. The default is 5950.

---

**NOTE**

It is important to understand the difference between Remote Control and Remote Login. Remote Control performs what you would traditionally expect: viewing the user's desktop and having control over the mouse and keyboard. Remote Login, however, launches a new login session (much like a terminal server), which prompts you for a login and then creates a new desktop based on the username and password you provide. You have your own desktop and are not controlling any other user's desktop.

---

Select the OK button to perform the requested remote management operation. You can configure various options (ports, whether to prompt the user, and so on) on remote control by making settings changes under the Remote Management section. See Chapter 6, "System Settings" for more information.

# Imaging a Device

There is value in an organization having a standard image to be applied to Linux devices, both servers and workstations. This often can be most valuable when it comes to diagnostics and repair of a device with problems. The administrator may work to repair a user's workstation, for example, and if after a specified time a repair cannot be completed, it is often most effective to just reimage the device.

ZENworks Linux Management enables you to take and apply images onto devices. Before you can take an image using PXE, you must have the novell-proxydhcp running on the ZENworks server. If you want to take an image from booting a CD or from booting a ZENworks partition on the device, you just need to make sure that the imaging server (pbserv) and the novell-zmgprebootproxy server is running.

This can be set to run though the YAST tool modifying runlevels for each individual service.

The taking of an image can be done either automatically through ZENworks Control Center or manually from the device. The following sections describe how this can be accomplished.

# Taking an Image from ZENworks Control Center

An image can be taken from a device after it has been registered with the ZENworks Zone. Execute the following to take an image of a registered device:

1. Launch ZENworks Control Center.

2. Log in as an administrator.

3. Browse to the device with the image you want to take.

4. Click the Take Image quick task. You are presented with a File Information screen (see Figure 11.4).

**FIGURE 11.4**
File Information page for taking an image.

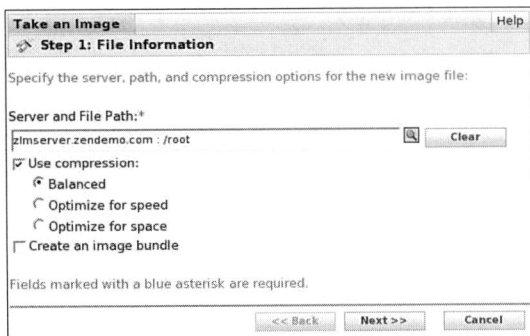

5. Enter the Server address or DNS name and the file path to a directory in the Server and File Path field. You can do so by pressing the browse button next to the field and entering the information. Press Next.

6. Review the summary page and press Finish.

7. A work order now has been created in the system to take an image of the device the next time the device is booted. Rebooting the device can be done via Remote Control or manually on the device.

8. Boot the device to the network, using PXE or another ZENworks imaging boot method. This causes the system to connect to the ZENworks Linux Management imaging system installed with the product. The system knows the device and recognizes that a work order has been created to take an image of the device.

9. The system then brings down a Linux kernel used for imaging and takes an image of the device, placing the resulting file at the path specified.

## Taking an Image Manually

You can take an image of a device manually at any time. You can do so by booting from a CD/DVD or from the network, using the components previously described.

If you are going to take a manual image via CD/DVD, you must first create the CD/DVD. This can be accomplished by burning the .iso image (`/opt/novell/zenworks/zdm/imaging/winutils/bootcd.iso`) from the ZENworks server onto a CD or DVD. Configuration options can be manipulated via a `settings.txt` file on the CD.

To manually take an image of a device, do the following:

1. Boot from the network. When the device gets its DHCP address, press and hold the Ctrl-Alt keys until the ZENworks menu comes up. Choose ZENworks Maintenance Mode Imaging from the menu.

   or

   Insert the CD you created in the earlier steps and boot from the CD. When the menu comes up, choose the Manual Mode option.

**NOTE**

You can control the menu choices that are available on the ZENworks menu through zone settings administered on the Configurations page. See Chapter 9, "Policies," for more information.

2. After the Linux system has booted, you come to a standard `bash#` prompt. At this point you can run the local interface by typing **img**.

3. Follow the options to create an image and have it placed on a server or on a local partition.

# Restoring an Image to a Device

Restoring an image that has been taken previously can be done via ZENworks Control Center or manually.

To restore an image from the ZENworks Control Center, execute the following:

1. Launch the ZENworks Control Center.
2. Log in as an administrator.
3. Create a reboot bundle. See Chapter 7, "Bundles," for more information.

4. Assign the bundle to the device.

5. Browse to the device in the ZENworks Control Center.

6. Press the Advanced menu item on the Preboot Work snapshot on the screen. See Figure 11.5 for a sample screen.

**FIGURE 11.5**
Sample screen of a Preboot Work advanced page.

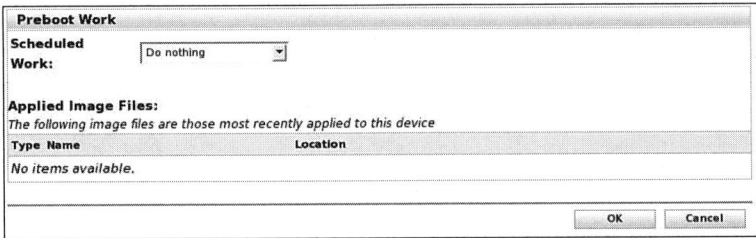

7. Select the drop-down list on the Scheduled Work field and select Apply Preboot Bundle. This displays something like Figure 11.6 on the page.

**FIGURE 11.6**
Sample screen of a Preboot Work advance page with Apply selected.

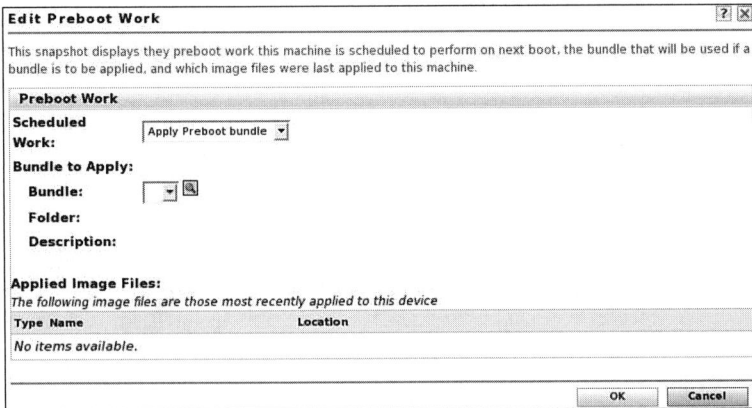

8. Browse to and select the preboot bundle that represents the image you want to apply to this device by selecting the Browse button next to the bundle field.

9. Press OK.

10. Now reboot the device to PXE, and ZENworks places that image down onto the device.

To restore an image manually, insert the same CD that you created in the "Taking an Image Manually" section and request through the interface to have the image placed on the device.

# ZENworks Partition

There are older machines that do not support PXE and therefore cannot get images from the network in a pre–operating system boot environment. For these machines, ZENworks offers the capability to place a ZENworks partition on the local machine, which holds the Linux pre–operating system boot environment that would normally be sent to the device over PXE.

When a ZENworks partition is placed on the device, the hardware first boots to the ZENworks partition that is to load the Linux environment and checks with the ZENworks Imaging server to see whether the system has been configured to take or restore an image to the system. This provides the automated capabilities of image management without the need for PXE.

To install a ZENworks partition on the device, complete the following steps:

1. Create a boot CD of the ZENworks boot system by burning the `.iso` image (`/opt/novell/zenworks/zdm/imaging/winutils/bootcd.iso`) from the ZENworks server onto a CD or DVD. Configuration options can be manipulated via a `settings.txt` file on the CD.

2. Boot the device with the ZENworks Imaging CD.

3. Select Install/Update ZEN Partition from the presented menu.

4. If the Imaging Server address is not specified in the `settings.txt` included in the CD, enter the IP address of the server, when prompted.

5. The system then creates the partition and installs the Linux boot environment into that partition. When completed, the system prompts you to remove the CD and reboot.

This adds the ZENworks partition, which checks at each reboot to see whether there is any administered preboot work for the device. If so, the device performs that work and then boots into the operating system.

.

# CHAPTER 12

# Keeping ZENworks Linux Management Servers Synchronized

This chapter discusses how to keep all your ZENworks servers (both primary and secondary) synchronized with object and package data. Additionally, this chapter discusses how to keep the primary server synchronized with an external source stream of updates for your Linux systems.

## Content Replication

Under the zone Configuration page is a category called Content Replication. This category represents the settings that are available in ZENworks Linux Management for sending administered content throughout the system.

Content replication in ZENworks Linux Management uses ZENworks Tiered Electronic Distribution.

### ZENworks Tiered Electronic Distribution

ZENworks Linux Management takes advantage of a transmission technology that was originally developed by the traditional ZENworks product line. This technology allows for very efficient and controlled distribution of content to any server in the network.

Tiered Electronic Distribution (TED) is used by ZENworks Linux Management to effectively transmit all RPM packages from the ZENworks primary server to all secondary servers. For example,

TED transmits to secondary servers only updates to the RPM packages, and does not send any packages that have already been copied to the secondary servers.

TED also has a check-point restart feature, where if the connection drops between the source and destination server, TED resumes the content transmission when the connection is restored, without retransmitting any data that was already sent.

**NOTE**

TED synchronizes content only one way: from the source to the target servers. That is why package management in ZENworks Linux Management must be done on the primary server. It always is treated as the source, whereas all secondary servers are considered the targets.

## Configuring Synchronization

To configure when ZENworks should synchronize the secondary servers with the package content on the primary server, execute the following steps:

1. Open ZENworks Control Center in your browser.

2. Log in as an administrator.

3. Click on the Configuration tab at the top of the ZENworks Control Center. This brings up the Management Zone Settings page. See Figure 12.1 for a sample page.

4. Click on the Content Replication setting. This brings up the page to make this setting. See Figure 12.2 for an example.

5. Click on the desired schedule type. The options include the following:

   - No Schedule
   - Date Specific
   - Day of the Week Specific
   - Monthly

   The various scheduling types are described in more detail in the following sections.

6. Select Close to have the schedule applied.

**FIGURE 12.1**
Sample Management Zone Setting page.

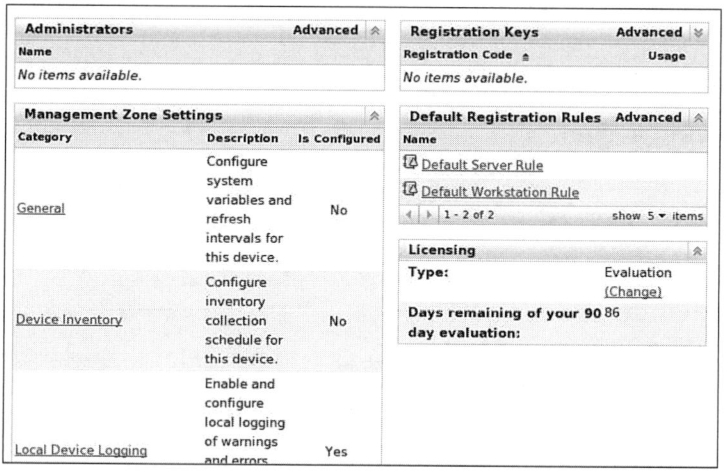

| Administrators | | Advanced ☆ |
|---|---|---|
| **Name** | | |
| No items available. | | |

| Registration Keys | Advanced ☆ |
|---|---|
| **Registration Code** ☆ | **Usage** |
| No items available. | |

| Management Zone Settings | | ☆ |
|---|---|---|
| **Category** | **Description** | **Is Configured** |
| General | Configure system variables and refresh intervals for this device. | No |
| Device Inventory | Configure inventory collection schedule for this device. | No |
| Local Device Logging | Enable and configure local logging of warnings and errors | Yes |

| Default Registration Rules Advanced ☆ |
|---|
| **Name** |
| 🗎 Default Server Rule |
| 🗎 Default Workstation Rule |
| ◁ ▷ 1 - 2 of 2          show 5 ▾ items |

| Licensing | ☆ |
|---|---|
| **Type:** | Evaluation (Change) |
| **Days remaining of your 90 day evaluation:** | 86 |

**FIGURE 12.2**
Example of the Content Replication settings page.

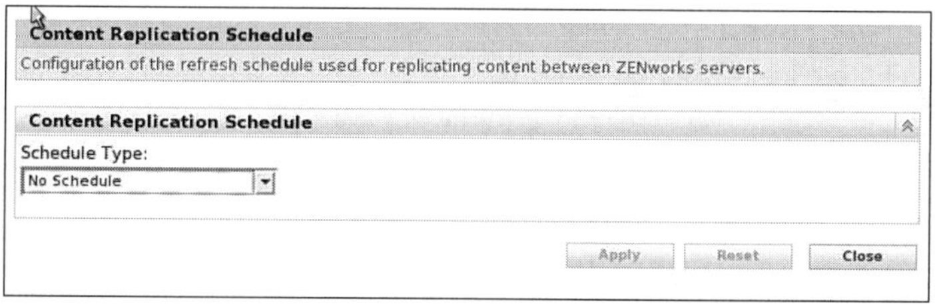

| Content Replication Schedule |
|---|
| Configuration of the refresh schedule used for replicating content between ZENworks servers. |

| Content Replication Schedule | ☆ |
|---|---|
| Schedule Type: | |
| No Schedule ▾ | |

Apply    Reset    **Close**

After the scheduled event occurs, ZENworks dynamically creates a TED relationship between the primary server and the secondary servers. Then it gathers all changed or new packages, compresses them, and sends them to the secondary servers.

The secondary servers, after they receive the compressed content, extract the files and place them appropriately on the secondary server.

# No Schedule Type

The No Schedule type prohibits content replication from occurring. This is the default schedule when the ZENworks Linux Management system is installed.

# Date Specific Schedule Type

With the Date Specific schedule type you can identify a selected date or dates in the year when you want this action to occur. When you select Date Specific, the screen displays the page illustrated in Figure 12.3.

**FIGURE 12.3**
Date Specific scheduling page.

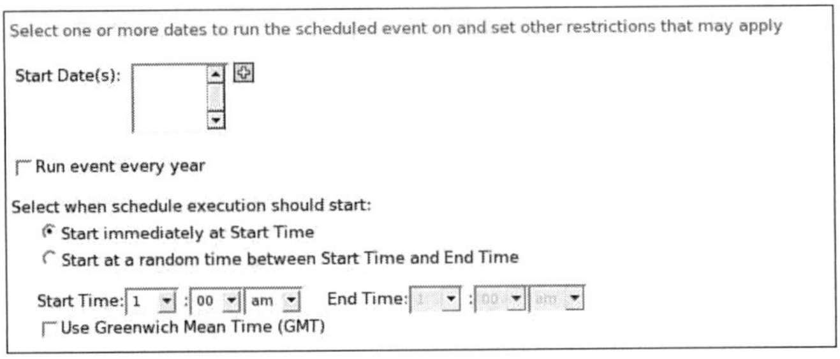

On the Date Specific schedule page you can enter the following information:

- **Start Dates**—Press the plus icon. This brings up the pop-up calendar dialog (see Figure 12.4) where you can select the date you want. To change the month, click on the diamond next to the month. To change the year, click on the diamond next to the year. After you have selected your date, the dialog automatically closes and the selected date appears in the Start Dates list.

**FIGURE 12.4**
Date Picker dialog for selecting a specific date of the year.

To remove the date, select the date in the Start Dates and press the minus icon.

■ **Run Event Every Year**—Select the check box to cause content replication to occur every year on the selected dates.

■ **Select When Schedule Execution Should Start**—In this area you can select whether the replication should occur at the given start time, or whether the execution should occur randomly between a given start and end time.

Enter the start time when you want the replication to begin. Enter the stop time, if you selected that the execution should occur randomly.

Select whether the time entered should be interpreted as Greenwich Mean Time (or Universal Time). Otherwise the system assumes you mean the local time of the primary server.

## Day of the Week Specific Schedule Type

The Day of the Week schedule enables you to select a particular day of the week, along with some time schedules when you want the content replication to occur. Complete the following sections to identify your day of the week schedule. Figure 12.5 is an example of this type of schedule.

**FIGURE 12.5**
Day of the Week Specific schedule page.

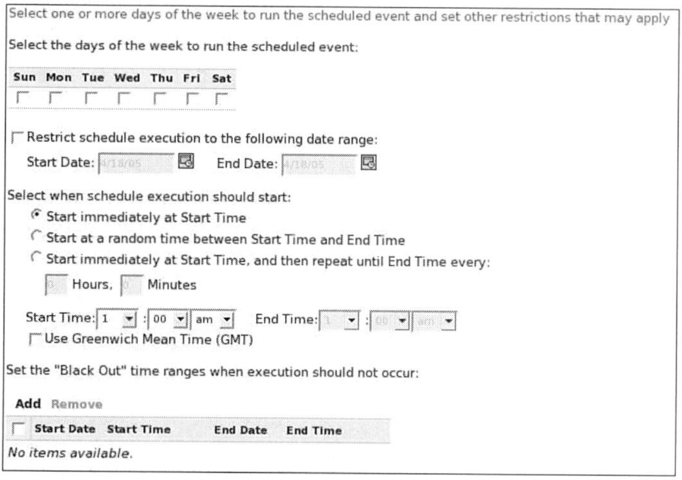

## SELECT THE DAYS OF THE WEEK

The first items to select are the days of the week when you want the content replication processes to run. Select the days of the week by clicking on the check box under your desired days.

## RESTRICT SCHEDULE TO THE FOLLOWING DATE RANGE

Select the Restrict Schedule Execution to the Following Date Range check box if you want the system to perform the scheduled activity only during a specified calendar range. Then enter a start and end date by selecting the calendar browse button and picking the date on the pop-up calendar view.

## SELECT WHEN SCHEDULE EXECUTION SHOULD START

This area enables you to select the time or time range when you want the content replication process to begin, on the days that you have specified earlier.

Choose one of the following options:

- **Start Immediately at Start Time**—This activates the content replication system at the specified start time.

- **Start at a Random Time Between Start Time and End Time**—This choice generates a random time that is between the start and end times. Then the content replication process begins at that randomly selected time.

- **Start Immediately at Start Time, and Then Repeat Until End Time**— This option starts the content replication process at the specified start time. Then it relaunches the content replication process at the interval specified in the Hours and Minutes fields. The system continues to relaunch the process at the interval specified until the end time is reached.

### NOTE

Subsequent launches of the content replication process result in only files that have changed since the previous replication process being sent to the secondary server.

Next, specify your start time and end time. Select the hour and minutes from the drop-down list and then choose a.m. or p.m. Enter in both the start and end times.

Next, if the time you have specified is a Greenwich Mean Time or Universal Time rather than the local time of the primary server, check the check box next to the Use Greenwich Mean Time (GMT) option.

## SET THE "BLACK OUT" TIME RANGES WHEN EXECUTION SHOULD NOT OCCUR

This option enables you to specify time ranges, which may fall within a calculated Start and End time. For example, imagine that you like to update your content every Saturday of the month. However, at the end of each business quarter you want your servers to work on end-of-quarter activities and not consume cycles transmitting package content. You can make this happen by entering your schedule and then selecting blackout dates for the end of each quarter. This way, if the calculated start time occurs within a specified blackout date, ZENworks does not launch the replication process. The content replication process is not started again until the next schedule time.

To enter blackout dates, complete the following:

1. Press the Add menu item. A pop-up dialog box is presented (see Figure 12.6).

**FIGURE 12.6**
Pop-up dialog to enter blackout dates and times.

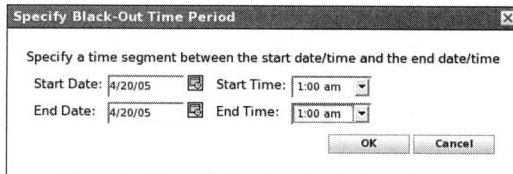

2. Enter the start date for the blackout period by selecting the calendar icon next to the Start Date field. This brings up the calendar pop-up, where you can select your date.

3. Enter the start time when the blackout period will begin on the start date by clicking on the drop-down list next to this field and selecting a specific hour of the day.

4. Enter the end date for the blackout period. This is initialized to be the same date as the chosen start date.

5. Enter the time when the blackout period will end on the end date by selecting an hour from the drop-down list.

6. Press the OK button to have the time entered as a blackout specification.

The entered blackout period is displayed on the screen. The blackout period begins at the specified time on the start date and ends at the selected end time on the end date.

To remove previously entered blackout periods, select the check box next to the listed blackout period and then click on the Remove menu item.

# Monthly Schedule Type

The Monthly Schedule enables you to select which days of each month you want the content replication process to be launched.

First select the day of the month when you want the process to begin. This is done by choosing one of the following:

- Start the scheduled event on a specific day of the month. This option starts the content replication on the given day of the month. Enter the numerical day of each month when you want the process to run.

- Start the scheduled event on the last day of the month. This option starts the process on the last day of the current month.

Now select the time or time range when you want the content replication process to begin.

Choose one of the following options:

- **Start Immediately at Start Time**—This activates the content replication system at the specified start time.

- **Start at a Random Time Between Start Time and End Time**—This choice generates a random time that is between the start and end times. Then the content replication process begins at that randomly selected time.

Next, specify your start time and end time. This is accomplished by selecting the hour and minute from the drop-down list and then choosing a.m. or p.m. Enter in both the start and end times.

Next, if the time you have specified is a Greenwich Mean Time or Universal Time, rather than the local time of the primary server, check the check box next to the Use Greenwich Mean Time (GMT) option.

Now you can set out blackout times for your content replication.

The Black Out option enables you to specify time ranges, which may fall within a calculated Start and End time. If the calculated start time occurs within a specified blackout date, then ZENworks does not launch the replication process. The content replication process is not started again until the next schedule time.

To enter blackout dates, complete the following:

**1.** Press the Add menu item. A pop-up dialog box is presented (refer to Figure 12.6).

**2.** Enter the start date for the blackout period by selecting the calendar icon next to the Start Date field. This brings up the calendar pop-up, where you can select your date.

**3.** Enter the start time when the blackout period begins on the start date by clicking on the drop-down list next to this field and selecting a specific hour of the day.

**4.** Enter the end date for the blackout period. This is initialized to be the same date as the chosen start date.

**5.** Enter the time when the blackout period will end on the end date by selecting an hour from the drop-down list.

**6.** Press the OK button to have the time entered in as a blackout specification.

The entered blackout period is displayed on the screen. The blackout period will begin at the specified time on the start date and will end at the selected end time on the end date.

To remove previously entered blackout periods, select the check box next to the listed blackout period and then click on the Remove menu item.

# Mirroring External Sources into ZENworks Linux Management

Patches and updates from various Linux sources are published on the Internet. For large deployments, you also may have several ZENworks Linux Management zones in your environment. Mirroring enables you to have ZENworks retrieve large numbers of packages from an external source hosted outside of your network, such as from the Internet or from outside your local zone.

Using mirroring, you can maintain updated packages for operating systems such as SUSE LINUX and SLES LINUX as well as Red Hat systems. With mirroring you can also share catalogs and bundles between two independent zones.

Mirroring is accomplished through the use of configuration files and a command-line tool called `zlmmirror`. To schedule mirroring to occur on a regular basis, you need to configure a CRON entry and schedule when the `zlmmirror` command should run.

The `zlmmirror` usage process typically works in the following fashion:

1. The system administrator creates a configuration file (or converts a previously existing ZENworks Linux Management configuration file) called `zlmmirrorconf.xml`, which details specifics of the remote and local servers, as well as which catalogs, bundles, and packages are to be copied. The `zlmmirrorconf.xml` file should be located in the /etc/opt/novell/zenworks directory.

2. System administrators set a cron entry or other scheduled time for `zlmmirror` to run.

3. Using the `zlmmirrorconf.xml` file, `zlmmirror` determines what catalog data to request from the servers.

4. `zlmmirror` authenticates to the remote server and downloads information about selected catalogs.

5. `zlmmirror` authenticates to the local server as a standard client, and downloads information about those same catalogs.

6. Catalog data from the remote and local servers is compared with the package and target filtering information from `zlmmirrorconf.xml`, to determine which packages need to be downloaded.

7. Packages are downloaded from the remote server.

8. `zlmmirror` authenticates to the local ZENworks Linux Management server as an administrator and adds the packages to the server in the appropriate bundles, creating catalogs as necessary.

Now let's take a closer look into the `zlmmirrorconf.xml` file.

## Looking at the `zlmmirrorconf.xml` File

The `zlmmirrorconf.xml` file describes the URL locations of the source servers that will be providing the information to the local primary server running the `zlmmirror` command. Additionally, the `zlmmirrorconf.xml` file configures which catalogs or channels should be retrieved and how to place the packages from these sources into ZENworks Linux Management.

For mirroring to function, you must define a single source server (you can have only one) and a single destination server (only one here, too). You can then define any number of catalog configurations that describe how the source server's content should be mapped into your ZENworks Linux Management server.

Because there are times when you want to mirror from many different sites, zlmmirror takes a config file as a parameter. If no parameter is specified, zlmmirror uses the default zlmmirrorconf.xml file. If you want to mirror from multiple sources, create a configuration file for mirroring from each source, and then create a cron job that launches zlmmirror with the desired config file for each source you want to mirror.

## SOURCE SERVER DEFINITION

The following template is used to define the source server:

```
<SourceServer>
    <Base>http://red-carpet.ximian.com/</Base>
    <Type>rce</Type>
    <User />
    <Password />
</SourceServer>
```

The Base path to the server you want to mirror must be in one of the following formats, depending on the type:

- For ZENworks Linux Management sources, use the format of https:// server
- For Red Carpet Enterprise servers, use the format of https://server/path
- For YAST updates, use the format of http(s)://server/path or ftp://server/path
- For Red Hat Network updates, use the format of http(s)://server/path

The type of server must be one of the following specifications:

- ZLM for ZENworks 7 Linux Management Servers
- RCE for Red Carpet Enterprise or ZENworks 6.x Linux Management systems
- YAST for YAST Online Update servers
- RHN for Red Hat Network systems

The user is the name of an account that has rights to read the packages and information from the source server. The Password field is the corresponding password for the user account.

The User is the name of an administrator account that has rights to write and create the bundles and catalogs into the destination server. If no user is specified, `zlmmirror` reads the identity from the following files, depending on the type:

- ZENworks 7 Linux Management: /etc/opt/novell/zenworks/zmd/deviceid
- Red Carpet Enterprise or ZENworks 6.x Linux Management: /etc/ximian/mcookie
- YAST: /etc/sysconfig/onlineupdate
- Red Hat Network: Leave the username empty in the form.

`zlmmirror` reads the following locations for the password portion of the form:

- ZENworks 7 Linux Management: /etc/opt/novell/zenworks/zmd/secret
- Red Carpet Enterprise or ZENworks 6.x Linux Management: /etc/ximian/partnernet
- YAST: /etc/sysconfig/onlineupdate
- Red Hat Network: Leave the password empty in the form.

## DESTINATION SERVER DESCRIPTION

You must use the following format to describe the destination server:

```
<DestinationServer>
    <Base>https://localhost</Base>
    <Type>zlm</Type>
    <User>Administrator</User>
    <Password>password</Password>
</DestinationServer>
```

The User is the name of an administrator account that has rights to write and create the bundles and catalogs into the destination server. If no user is specified, `zlmmirror` reads the identity from the same files as specified in the preceding section.

The Base path in the form needs to be of the format of https://server for ZENworks 7 Linux Management and /path/on/filesystem for STATIC types, where the mirroring just copies the packages to the file system.

## CATALOG AND BUNDLE CONFIGURATION

You need to provide details on the catalogs and bundles you want mirrored to the ZENworks Linux Management server. This is defined in the catalog configuration form. Each catalog you want to mirror must have a separate CatalogConf section, as follows:

```
<CatalogConf>
    <Name>Red Carpet 2</Name>
    <LocalName>Red Carpet 2</LocalName>
    <Target>sles-9-i586</Target>
    <ExcludeTarget></ExcludeTarget>
    <Bundle></Bundle>
    <ExcludeBundle></ExcludeBundle>
    <Package>lib.*</Package>
    <ExcludePackage></ExcludePackage>
</CatalogConf>
```

The Name field is the name of the catalog or channel you want to mirror from this source server. This is the only required parameter. If it is not specified, zlmmirror creates or places the packages in a catalog with the same name.

Local Name field is the name of the catalog in which you want the mirrored software placed. If no local name is specified, the catalog name from the source server is used.

Folder specifies the object database folder (for example, /folder1/folder2) where bundles and catalogs are created and updated. If not specified, the catalogs and bundles will be created and updated in a /zlmmirror folder.

Target restricts the mirroring operation on this catalog to packages and patches that support the specified target platform(s). If no target is specified, packages for all platforms are mirrored. This element can be specified multiple times, and can contain either a target name or a regular expression string for wildcard matching of target names.

ExcludeTarget is the same as Target, except packages and patches supporting the specified target platform(s) are excluded.

ExcludeBundle is performed after Target, so platforms appearing in a Target and ExcludeTarget are ultimately excluded.

Bundle restricts the mirroring operation on this catalog to the specified bundle(s). If not specified, all bundles are mirrored. This option is valid only for ZENworks Linux Management and YAST source servers. It can be specified multiple times and can contain either a bundle name or a regular expression string for wildcard matching of bundle names.

ExcludeBundle is the same as Bundle, except packages and patches contained in the specified bundle(s) are excluded. This option is valid only for ZENworks Linux Management and YAST source servers. It can be specified multiple times and can contain either a bundle name or a regular expression string for wild-card matching of bundle names. ExcludeBundle is performed after Bundle, so bundles appearing in a Bundle and ExcludeBundle are ultimately excluded.

Package restricts the mirroring operation on this catalog to the specified package(s). If not specified, all package(s) are mirrored. This option is valid only for ZENworks Linux Management and YAST source servers. It can be specified multiple times and can contain either a bundle name or a regular expression string for wildcard matching of bundle names.

ExcludePackage is the same as Package, except specified package(s) are excluded. This option is valid only for ZENworks Linux Management and YAST source servers. It can be specified multiple times and can contain either a bundle name or a regular expression string for wildcard matching of bundle names. ExcludePackage is performed after Package, so packages appearing in a Package and ExcludePackage are ultimately excluded.

## EXAMPLE CONFIGURATION

The following displays a typical configuration file to mirror an NLD catalog from zone1 to zone2.

```
<ZLMMirrorConf>
  <SourceServer>
  <Base>https://sourceprimary.zone1.com</Base>
  <Proxy />
  <Type>zlm</Type>
  <User>Administrator</User>
  <Password>source</Password>
</SourceServer>

<DestinationServer>
  <Base>https://localhost</Base>
  <Type>zlm</Type>
  <User>Administrator</User>
  <Password>target</Password>
</DestinationServer>

<CatalogConf>
  <Name nld-9-i586/>
  <LocalName nld-9-i586/>
  <Folder Mirror/>
  <Target />
  <ExcludeTarget />
  <Bundle />
  <ExcludeBundle />
  <Package />
```

```
    <ExcludePackage />
  </CatalogConf>

  </ZLMMirrorConf>
```

This configuration file causes the nld-9-i586 catalog to be copied and updated on the local primary server. The local catalog name will also be nld-9-586 and will exist in the /Bundles/Mirror folder of the ZENworks Control Center.

## Finishing Up the Configuration

You should test your configuration file to see whether it is formed properly and will perform the intended actions.

After you have created the configuration file for a source server, run the following command to perform a dry run of the mirroring operation, and optionally add the verbose flag to see detailed messages:

```
zlmmirror mirror -c zlmmirror-config.xml --dryrun -verbose
```

If this operation provides the intended results, run the `mirror` command without the dry run flag to complete the operation:

```
zlmmirror mirror -c zlmmirror-config.xml
```

After you have configured your system and created your cron entries, `zlmmirror` continually refreshes your local catalogs with the latest updates.

See Appendix A, "Commands," for all the options that are available for the `zlmmirror` command.

# Summary

It is important when you have more than one server in your ZENworks Linux Management to keep your servers synchronized with the files and administered functions. Additionally, to bring outside packages into the system automatically, you need to set up configurations and jobs for each mirroring activity you want.

Using these techniques brings content into your system that you can then provide to your devices via catalogs or assign for installation to devices through assignments of bundles.

# CHAPTER 13

# ZENworks Linux Management Database

This chapter discusses the database used for ZENworks Linux Management.

## ZENworks Linux Management Databases

By default, ZENworks Linux Management installs PostgreSQL version 7.4.7. However, you can also use Oracle 9i. During the install, you are prompted whether you want to install the database locally (on the machine on which you are installing ZENworks Linux Management) or to a remote PostgreSQL or Oracle database.

ZENworks Linux Management also uses an object store. The ZENworks Object Store is eDirectory. It's important to understand that unlike relational databases, the ZENworks Object Store can establish interrelationships of data, such as the relationship of an application to a workstation.

## Information Stored in the Database

The ZENworks 7 Linux Management database contains a lot of information used by the product. The following information is found in only the database:

- Log Files
- Inventory
- Queue information
- Package and bundle dependency

The following information is found in only the ZENworks Object Store:

- Administrators/Users
- Policies
- Tiered Electronic Distribution (TED) Configuration

The following information is stored in both the ZENworks Object Store and the database:

- Registration information
- Package information (bundles, catalogs, and so on)

# Accessing PostgreSQL

You should never have to change or modify the database directly. However, you can use a few commands to look at the information within the database. If you used the defaults to set up ZENworks Linux Management, you can access PostgreSQL by following these steps:

1. At the terminal prompt type **su postgres**.

2. Type **psql zenworks** to log in to the database.

   You then see the following information:

   ```
   Welcome to psql 7.4.7, the PostgreSQL interactive terminal.
   Type:    \copyright for distribution terms
   \h for help with SQL commands
   \? for help on internal slash commands
   \g or terminate with semicolon to execute query
   \q to quit

   zenworks=#
   ```

3. Type **\d** to view a description of what is in the database.

   You see a screen similar to Figure 13.1.

**FIGURE 13.1**
List of relations for PostgreSQL database.

```
                   List of relations
 Schema |         Name          |  Type    |  Owner
--------+-----------------------+----------+----------
 public | action_arg            | table    | postgres
 public | batchemistry_enum     | table    | postgres
 public | battery               | table    | postgres
 public | bios                  | table    | postgres
 public | bundle_deps           | table    | postgres
 public | bundle_package        | table    | postgres
 public | bundle_world          | table    | postgres
 public | bundles               | table    | postgres
 public | bus                   | table    | postgres
 public | bustype_enum          | table    | postgres
 public | cdrom                 | table    | postgres
 public | chassis               | table    | postgres
 public | chassistype_enum      | table    | postgres
 public | dependency_type       | table    | postgres
 public | desktop_monitor       | table    | postgres
 public | driver                | table    | postgres
 public | eventparam            | view     | postgres
 public | file_dependency       | table    | postgres
 public | floppy_disk           | table    | postgres
 public | hibernate_sequence    | sequence | postgres
lines 1-23
```

4. You can also type **\d <value>** to see details about a specific item in the database. For example, if you type **\d battery** you will see a screen similar to Figure 13.2.

**FIGURE 13.2**
Description of battery table.

```
                  Table "public.battery"
     Column      |         Type          | Modifiers
-----------------+-----------------------+----------
 batteryid       | bigint                | not null
 name            | character varying(128) |
 chemistry       | smallint              |
 design_capacity | smallint              |
 design_voltage  | smallint              |
 smart_bat_version| character varying(32) |
 manufacturer    | character varying(128) |
 serial_number   | character varying(64) |
 hwid            | bigint                |
Indexes:
    "battery_pkey" primary key, btree (batteryid)
    "battery_hwid_idx" btree (hwid)
Foreign-key constraints:
    "battery_hwid_fk" FOREIGN KEY (hwid) REFERENCES zen_machine(hwid)
```

In addition to the listed commands , you can manage the information from the database by using the ZENworks Control Center, or using commands in zlman.

# Where to Get More Information

You can get excellent information, documentation, and so on for PostgreSQL at www.postgresql.org.

You can get more information about the ZENworks Object Store (eDirectory 8.7.3) at http://www.novell.com/documentation/edir873/index.html.

# Conclusion

ZENworks Linux Management provides robust capabilities for storing and managing your Linux systems. Whether you choose PostgreSQL or Oracle, you will have the enterprise tools and power you've come to expect from Novell.

# CHAPTER 14

# Troubleshooting

ZENworks Linux Management is a powerful tool that can be used to manage and update your Linux devices. However, because of the complexity of network environments, problems can occur that prevent ZENworks from doing its job. This chapter covers how to troubleshoot problems in the ZENworks Linux Management system.

## Registering and Un-registering a Device

There may be occasions when you need to un-register your workstation from the zone. With the local **rug** command you can un-register and then re-register a device to the desired zone.

To un-register a device, do the following:

1. Go to a command-line interface on the device.

2. Enter the **rug sl** command to see all the services against which this device is registered. Note the number of the service that you want to remove (this is the number in the first column of the output).

3. Enter the following command to un-register from the service: **rug sd <Number of the Service>**.

This removes the service. If the service is a ZENworks Linux Management service and you had registered it before, the act of un-registering does not remove the device in the object store. If you want to remove the device object, you must delete it in the ZENworks Control Center.

To register a device, do the following:

1. Go to a command-line interface on the device.

2. Enter the **rug sl** command to see all the services against which this device is registered. Check that you have not registered to the desired server. If you have, you need to un-register first.

3. Enter the following command to register from the service: **rug sa <DNS or Address of ZENworks server>**.

This registers your device to the ZENworks zone of that server. The act of registering makes a device object in the system.

# Creating Custom Platforms

On occasion, you may have some special custom distributions that your company has created based on one of the supported platforms of ZENworks Linux Management. These custom distributions can be recognized by ZENworks, and then RPMs in the bundles can have the new custom distributions as targets, enabling you to identify that the RPM is for those device types only.

To create a new custom platform, complete the following:

1. Launch ZENworks Control Center.

2. Select the Configuration tab at the top of the browser.

3. Select Platforms from the Management Zone Settings.

4. Scroll to the bottom of the screen and select Add from the Custom Target Platforms snapshot. You are presented with the dialog box shown in Figure 14.1.

**FIGURE 14.1**
Add Platform dialog for creating custom target platforms.

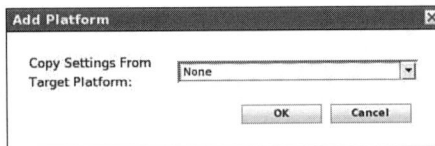

5. The simplest way to fill in the custom platforms is to copy a default platform that is similar to your custom system and then edit the contents. Select a similar platform by clicking on the drop-down menu list and selecting an existing target platform. Press OK.

6. You are presented next with the Add Platform dialog, with the fields defaulted to your copied platform (see Figure 14.2). Edit the fields as desired.

**FIGURE 14.2**
Add Platform dialog box.

- **Name**—Enter the name of the platform as it is to be displayed in ZENworks Control Center.
- **Vendor**—Enter the vendor of the distribution.
- **Product Name**—Enter the product name of the distribution.
- **Version**—Enter the version number of the product.
- **Package Manager**—Enter the package manager for the platform.
- **Architecture**—Enter the architecture for the product.
- **Device Type**—Select whether the device with this product is a workstation or server.

- **OS Detection String**—Modify the XML strings in the box to point to the file on the device that would contain the release information and the string that the system must match to determine the platform of a device.

- **Enable This Platform**—Select the check box to enable this platform to be presented in menus and in other areas in the ZENworks Control Center.

7. Press OK. This adds this platform to the set understood by ZENworks.

Now this platform appears in your platform selection as part of adding RPMs to a bundle.

# Configuring Silent Installation of the Agent

You can run an installation of the agent and record your responses, placing them in a configuration file. Then you can re-use that configuration file for other agent installations. When you use the configuration file as an option to the agent installation, the installation is silent.

Record the installation by running `zlm-install -a -r <config file path>`. This creates a config file with your responses.

To play the installation on another workstation in silent mode, run `zlm-install -a -s <config file path>`. This installs the agent with the same configuration as specified in the recorded installation.

# Cleaning the Database

When an entry is removed in a Postgres database, the database marks the entry as invalid, but does not remove the entry from the database. There is a tool, `/opt/novell/zenworks/bin/zlm-pq-vacuum`, that can be run to purge the database of all removed items.

Run this tool periodically, or as a cron job to keep your database clean.

You should note that you may need to edit the `zlm-pq-vacuum` file to allow for silent execution of the tool. By following the instructions in the file you can have the tool bypass the prompt for the database password.

# Updating the Agent

There are times when you need to make sure that the agent running on the local device is updated with the latest agent code. This can be accomplished by running the **rug up** command.

This contacts the ZENworks Linux Management server, downloads the latest agent files, and installs them on the local device.

# Encrypting a VNC Session

The version of VNC that is shipped with ZENworks Linux Management does not currently encrypt the communication between the viewer and client (host) machine. Most administrators who want to remote control a GUI-less device use the **ssh** command to control the device remotely. If you need to run the VNC tool in graphical mode and still want to encrypt the session, complete the following steps:

1. Launch a terminal session on the administrator's device (viewer).
2. Launch the ZENworks Control Center and browse to the device you want to remote-control. Discover the device's IP address.
3. You need to set up a tunnel port connection between the ZCC device and the managed device you want to control. To do this you need three pieces of information:
   - The port on the ZENworks Control Center device that is free (assume 1234 for the example)
   - The port of the VNC server that is running on the target device (this is 5950 by default)
   - The IP address of the target device (should have gotten that in the previous step)

   Enter the following in the terminal session on the ZENworks Control Center device:

   ```
   ssh -L 1234:localhost:5950 <Target IP address>
   ```

   Optionally you can include -1 <user> to specify a user account. The SSH connection requires that you enter a password on a valid user account on the target device. As the shell makes a connection to the remote device, you are prompted for the password of the user you specified. After the password is supplied, the secure connection is finalized.

You can find out additional information on using SSH with VNC at http://www.uk.research.att.com/archive/vnc/sshvnc.html.

4. Go back to the ZENworks Control Center and click on the Devices tab.

5. Select the Remote Control Device task from the task list on the left. You are prompted with the following dialog (see Figure 14.3).

**FIGURE 14.3**
Remote Management dialog.

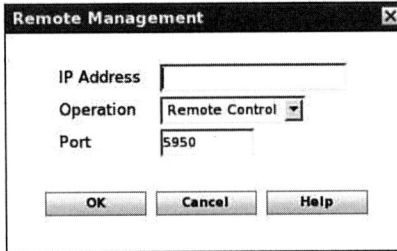

6. Enter **localhost** into the IP Address field.

7. Enter **1234** into the Port field.

8. Press OK. This starts the VNC viewer session over the tunneled port to the target device. Enter the password for the remote control session and press OK. This brings up the GUI of the device.

# Not Installing the VNC Agent

There may be times when, for security or space reasons, you may not want to have the agent install the VNC components that enable you to control the device remotely. You can do so by passing a -x option to the zlm-install command.

When the zlm-install command receives a -x option, no X-Windows components (namely VNC) are installed.

# Logging

By default, ZENworks Linux Management attempts to log lots of information and event data. You can configure the level of the logging on both the server and the device through zone settings. See Chapter 6, "System Settings," for more information about zone settings.

In ZENworks Linux Management, all logs are stored in a single location: `/var/opt/novell/log/zenworks`. Go to this directory to discover all the various logs that will contain information about the processes running on your system. Logs on the device may be found in the same location.

# Commands

This appendix discusses the command-line utilities for ZENworks Linux Management.

There are three different command line utilities:

zlman—This is the main utility for managing ZENworks Linux Management.

rug—This is the utility with which the agent on the managed device performs tasks such as install, update, remove software, and so on.

zlmmirror—This is the utility used to mirror bundles and catalogs, from remote ZENworks Linux Management, YAST Online Updates, and RedHat Network servers, to your local ZENworks Linux Management server or to a local directory.

Each command is labeled with the command name on the outer edge of the page. If there is a shortcut, it is displayed in parentheses next to the command. The syntax line is followed by a brief description and a list of any additional options.

## zlman

The following options are understood by all commands:

-?, --help—Get help on a specific command.

-U, --user=<*username*>—Specify username.

-P, --password=<*password*>—Specify password.

--log=<*logfile*>—Specify the file to which to log (default: /var/opt/novell/log/zenworks/zlman.log).

-d, --debug—Display debugging output.

--version—Print zlman version and exit.

-V, --verbose—Enable verbose output.

--quiet—Quiet output, print only error messages.

--ignore-rc-file—Ignore the ~/.zlmanrc file.

--host=<host>—Specify the hostname to which to connect (default: local-host).

--port=<port>—Specify the port on which the server is listening (default: 443).

--cleartext—Disable SSL for debugging purposes. Port must be set to the clear text port.

### SUMMARY OF ZLMAN COMMANDS

| command | usage/options | description |
|---|---|---|
| ping | zlman ping <options> | Verify that a server is operational and responsive. |
| registration-list (rl) | zlman registration-list <options><folder> <filter> | List all registrations. |
| | -f, --filter=<filter> | Display only options that match the specified filter. (Wild cards * and ? may be used if the filter is quoted.) |
| | -r, --recursive | Include objects in sub-folders. |
| registration-folder-create (rfc) | zlman registration-folder-create <options> <name> <folder> | Create a new folder. |
| registration-create-workstation (rcw) | zlman registration-create-workstation <options> <key> <folder> <device folder> | Create a new registration. A workstation folder may be specified. Workstations created with this registration are placed in this folder. |
| registration-create-server (rcs) | zlman registration-create-server <options> <key> <device folder> <folder> | Create a new registration. A server foldermay be specified. Servers created with this registration are placed in this folder. |
| registration-info (ri) | zlman registration-info <options> <key> | Display detailed information about a specific registration. |

**SUMMARY OF ZLMAN COMMANDS**  (continued)

| command | usage/options | description |
| --- | --- | --- |
| registration-list-groups (rlg) | zlman registration-list-groups *<options>* *<key>* | Display a list of the groups to which a device will be added when registered with the specified key. |
| registration-delete (rd) | zlman registration-delete *<options>* *<registration>* | Delete a registration. |
| registration-update (ru) | zlman registration-update *<options>* *<key>* | Update a registration. |
| | -k, --newkey=*<key>* | The new key value. |
| | -u, --usage=*<count>* | The maximum number of devices that can be created with this key. |
| | --unlimited | Remove the limit on the number of devices that can be created with this key. |
| | -n, --nrule=*<Naming Rule>* | Specify a new naming rule, such as ${HostName}. |
| | --workstation-folder=*<Folder>* | Specify the workstation folder in which an imported Workstation should be placed. |
| | --server-folder=*<Folder>* | Specify the server folder in which an imported Server should be placed. |
| registration-add-workstation-group (rawg) | zlman registration-add-workstation-group *<options>* *<key>* *<group>* | Add a Workstation Group membership to objects imported with a given key. |
| registration-add-server-group (rasg) | zlman registration-add-server-group *<options>* *<key>* *<group>* | Add a Server Group membership to objects imported with a given key. |
| registration-remove-workstation-group (rrwg) | zlman registration-remove-workstation-group *<options>* *<key>* *<group>* | Remove a Workstation Group membership from a registration. |
| registration-remove-server-group (rrsg) | zlman registration-remove-server-group *<options>* *<key>* *<group>* | Remove a Server Group membership from a registration. |

**SUMMARY OF ZLMAN COMMANDS** (continued)

| command | usage/options | description |
| --- | --- | --- |
| registration-move (rmv) | zlman registration-move <options> <key> <folder> | Move a registration to a different folder. |
| admin-list (al) | zlman admin-list <options> | Display a list of all administrators. |
| | -r, --recursive | Include objects in sub-folders. |
| | -f, --filter=<filter> | Display only options that match the specified filter. (Wild cards * and ? may be used, if the filter is quoted.) |
| admin-create (ac) | zlman admin-create <options> <admin name> <password> | Create a new administrator, with view-only rights to all objects. |
| admin-delete (ad) | zlman admin-delete <options> <admin name> | Delete an administrator. |
| admin-rename (arn) | zlman admin-rename <options> <admin name> <new name> | Rename an administrator. |
| admin-rights-get (arg) | zlman admin-rights-get <options> <admin name> <object name> | View the effective rights of a specific object. If no object is specified, all assigned rights are displayed. A single type flag must be specified. |
| | -w, --workstations | Specify that object is of type workstation. |
| | -s, --servers | Specify that object is of type server. |
| | -a, --administrators | Specify that object is of type administrator. |
| | -b, --bundles | Specify that object is of type bundle. |
| | -p, --policies | Specify that object is of type policy. |
| | -R, --reports | Specify that object is of type report. |
| | -r, --registrations | Specify that object is of type registration. |

**SUMMARY OF ZLMAN COMMANDS** (continued)

| command | usage/options | description |
|---|---|---|
| admin-rights-assign (ara) | zlman admin-rights-assign <options> <admin name> <object name> | View the effective rights of a specific object. If no object is specified, all assigned rights are displayed. A single type flag must be specified. |
| | -w, --workstations | Specify that object is of type workstation. |
| | -s, --servers | Specify that object is of type server. |
| | -a, --administrators | Specify that object is of type administrator. |
| | -b, --bundles | Specify that object is of type bundle. |
| | -p, --policies | Specify that object is of type policy. |
| | -R, --reports | Specify that object is of type report. |
| | -r, --registrations | Specify that object is of type registration. |
| | -n, --none | Remove all rights. |
| | -v, --view | Allow view only. |
| | -m, --modify | Allow modification of an object. |
| | -c, --create | Allow creation of new objects. |
| bundle-list (bl) | zlman bundle-list <options> <folder> <filter> | List bundles in a folder. |
| | -f, --filter=<filter> | Display only options that match the specified filter. (Wild cards * and ? may be used, if the filter is quoted.) |
| | -r, --recursive | Include objects in sub-folders. |
| bundle-create (bc) | zlman bundle-create <options> <name> <folder> | Create a new bundle. |

**SUMMARY OF ZLMAN COMMANDS** (continued)

| command | usage/options | description |
|---|---|---|
| bundle-folder-create (bfc) | zlman bundle-folder-create *<options>* *<name>* *<folder>* | Create a new folder for containing bundles. |
| bundle-delete (bd) | zlman bundle-delete *<options>* *<bundle>* | Delete one or more bundles. |
| bundle-rename (br) | zlman bundle-rename *<options>* *<name>* *<new name>* | Rename a bundle. |
| bundle-move (bmv) | zlman bundle-move *<options>* *<bundle>* *<folder>* | Move a bundle. |
| bundle-add-package (bap) | zlman bundle-add-package *<options>* *<bundle>* *<target>* *<package file>* | Add a package to a bundle. |
| | --installtype=*<install type>* | Specify rpm installation type. A value of "upgrade" indicates "rpm-U" behavior, and a value of "install" indicates "rpm -i" behavior. |
| bundle-copy-package (bcp) | zlman bundle-copy-package *<options>* *<<source bundle>>* *<<target bundle>>* *<target>* *<<package>>* *<package ID>* | Copy a package from one bundle to another bundle. |
| bundle-list-packages (blp) | zlman bundle-list-packages *<options>* *<bundle>* *<target>* | Display a list of packages contained by a bundle. |
| bundle-remove-package (brp) | zlman bundle-remove-package *<options>* *<bundle>* *<target>* *<package ID>* | Remove a package from a bundle. The package ID is listed with the bundle-list-packages command. |
| bundle-group-create (bgc) | zlman bundle-group-create *<options>* *<name>* *<folder>* | Create a bundle group. |
| bundle-group-members (bgl) | zlman bundle-group-members *<options>* *<group>* | List the members of a bundle group. |

**SUMMARY OF ZLMAN COMMANDS** (continued)

| command | usage/options | description |
| --- | --- | --- |
| bundle-group-<br>(bga) | zlman bundle-group-<br>add *<options> <group>*<br>*<bundle>* | Add a bundle to a bundle group. |
| bundle-group-<br>remove (bgr) | zlman bundle-group-<br>remove *<options>*<br>*<group> <bundle>* | Remove a bundle from a bundle group. |
| bundle-dep-<br>list (bdl) | zlman bundle-dep-list<br>*<options> <name>* | List dependencies for a bundle. |
| bundle-dep-<br>add (bda) | zlman bundle-dep-add<br>*<options> <name>*<br>*<dependency name>* | Add a dependency to a bundle. |
| bundle-dep-<br>remove (bdr) | zlman bundle-dep-<br>remove *<options>*<br>*<name> <dependency*<br>*name>* | Remove a dependency from a bundle. |
| patch-bundle-<br>create (pbc) | zlman patch-bundle-<br>create *<options>*<br>*<Product Name>*<br>*<Product Version>*<br>*<Product Arch>*<br>*<Patch File> <folder>* | Create a new patch bundle. |
| catalog-list (cl) | zlman catalog-list<br>*<options> <folder>*<br>*<filter>* | List catalogs in a folder. |
| | -r, --recursive | Include objects in sub-folders. |
| | -f, --filter=*<filter>* | Display only options that match the specified filter. (Wild cards * and ? may be used, if the filter is quoted.) |
| catalog-create<br>(cc) | zlman catalog-create<br>*<options> <name>*<br>*<folder>* | Create a new catalog. |
| catalog-folder-<br>create (cfc) | zlman catalog-folder-<br>create *<options>*<br>*<name> <folder>* | Create a new folder for containing catalogs. |
| catalog-delete<br>(cd) | zlman catalog-delete<br>*<options><catalog>* | Delete a catalog. |
| catalog-rename<br>(cr) | zlman catalog-rename<br>*<options> <name>*<br>*<new name>* | Rename a catalog. |

## SUMMARY OF ZLMAN COMMANDS (continued)

| command | usage/options | description |
| --- | --- | --- |
| catalog-move (cmv) | zlman catalog-move <options> <catalog> <folder> | Move a catalog. |
| catalog-list-bundles (clb) | zlman catalog-list-bundles <options> <catalog> | Display a list of all bundles associated with a catalog. |
| catalog-add-bundle (cab) | zlman catalog-add-bundle <options> <catalog> <bundle> | Associate a bundle with a catalog. |
| | --dry-run | |
| | -a, --allow-removal | |
| | --prepare-time=<HH:MM> | Specify a time of day at which the action should be performed. The time should be specified in the format "HH:MM," with hours in 24-hour format. |
| | --prepare-date=<YYYY-MM-DD> | Specify a specific date on which the action should be performed. The date should be specified in the format "YYYY-MM-DD." |
| | --time=<HH:MM> | Specify a time of day at which the action should be performed. The time should be specified in the format "HH:MM," with hours in 24-hour format. |
| | --date=<YYYY-MM-DD> | Specify a specific date on which the action should be performed. The date should be specified in the format "YYYY-MM-DD." |
| | --now | Specify that the action should be performed as soon as possible. A repeat frequency may be specified. If no other schedule is specified it defaults to now. |

**SUMMARY OF ZLMAN COMMANDS** (continued)

| command | usage/options | description |
| --- | --- | --- |
| | `--relative=<DD:HH:MM>` | Specify that the action should be performed at a time relative to now. The time should be formatted as "DD:HH:MM." A repeat frequency may be specified. |
| | `--weekly=<MWF>` | Specify the days of the week on which the action should be performed. If specified, the action is repeated every seven days. Example: "MWF" executes the action every Monday, Wednesday, and Friday. Monday = M, Tuesday = TU, Wednesday = W, Thursday = TH, Friday = F, Saturday = SA, Sunday = SU. |
| | `--monthly=<DD>` | Specify the day of the month on which the action should be performed. If specified, the action is repeated every month. Multiple days may not be specified. |
| | `--yearly=<MM-DD, MM-DD,...>` | Specify the days of the year on which the action should be performed. If specified, the action is repeated every year. Dates should be specified in the format "MM-DD." Multiple dates may be comma separated. |
| | `--repeat=<DD:HH:MM>` | Specify the repeat frequency for the action, in the format "DD:HH:MM." Days are optional. |
| | `--gmt` | All times given are treated as GMT. If not given, all times are treated as catalog-remove-bundle (crb). Remove the association between a bundle and a catalog. |

## SUMMARY OF ZLMAN COMMANDS    (continued)

| command | usage/options | description |
|---------|---------------|-------------|
| Catalog-remove-bundle (crb) | zlman catalog-remove-bundle <options> <catalog> <bundle> | Remove the association between a bundle and a catalog. |
| workstation-info (wi) | zlman workstation-info <options> <Workstation> | Display detailed information about a device. |
| workstation-list (wl) | zlman workstation-list <options> <folder> <filter> | List devices in a folder. |
| | -r, --recursive | Include objects in sub-folders. |
| | -f, --filter=<filter> | Display only options that match the specified filter. (Wild cards * and ? may be used, if the filter is quoted.) |
| workstation-messages (wm) | zlman workstation-messages <options> <Workstation> | Display a list of messages associated with the specified device. |
| | -a, --all | Display all messages, including those that have been acknowledged. |
| Workstation-ack (wa) | zlman workstation-ack <options> <Workstation> <Log ID> | Acknowledge a message associated with a device. |
| workstation-delete (wd) | zlman workstation-delete <options> <Workstation> | Delete one or more device, folder, or group. |
| workstation-refresh (wr) | zlman workstation-refresh <options> <Workstation> | Refresh the policies and bundles on one or more devices, folders, or groups. |
| | --Service=<Service> | Specify the name of the service to refresh on the device. If not given, all services are refreshed. |
| workstation-rename (wrn) | zlman workstation-rename <options> <Workstation> <New name> | Rename a device. |
| workstation-move (wmv) | zlman workstation-move <options> <Workstation> <folder> | Move a device to a different folder. |

**SUMMARY OF ZLMAN COMMANDS** (continued)

| command | usage/options | description |
|---|---|---|
| workstation-folder-create (wfc) | zlman workstation-folder-create *<options>* *<Name>* *<folder>* | Create a new folder. |
| workstation-group-create (wgc) | zlman workstation-group-create *<options>* *<Name>* *<folder>* | Create a new group. |
| workstation-group-members (wgm) | zlman workstation-group-members *<options>* *<Group>* | List members of a group. |
| workstation-group-add (wga) | zlman workstation-group-add *<options>* *<Group>* *<Workstation>* | Add one or more devices to a group. |
| workstation-group-remove (wgr) | zlman workstation-group-remove *<options>* *<Group>* *<Workstation>* | Remove one or more members of a group. |
| workstation-list-bundles (wlb) | zlman workstation-list-bundles *<options>* *<Workstation>* | List bundles associated with a device. |
| workstation-add-bundle (wab) | zlman workstation-add-bundle *<options>* *<Workstation>* *<bundle>* | Associate one or more bundles with a device. |
| | --dry-run | |
| | -a, --allow-removal | |
| | --prepare-time=*<HH:MM>* | Specify a time of day at which the action should be performed. The time should be specified in the format "HH:MM," with hours in 24-hour format. |
| | --prepare-date=*<YYYY-MM-DD>* | Specify a specific date on which the action should be performed. The date should be specified in the format "YYYY-MM-DD." |
| | --time=*<HH:MM>* | Specify a time of day at which the action should be performed. The time should be specified in the format "HH:MM," with hours in 24-hour format. |

## SUMMARY OF ZLMAN COMMANDS   (continued)

| command | usage/options | description |
|---|---|---|
| | `--date=<YYYY-MM-DD>` | Specify a specific date on which the action should be performed. The date should be specified in the format "YYYY-MM-DD." |
| | `--now` | Specify that the action should be performed as soon as possible. A repeat frequency may be specified. If no other schedule is specified it defaults to now. |
| | `--relative=<DD:HH:MM>` | Specify that the action should be performed at a time relative to now. The time should be formatted as "DD:HH:MM." A repeat frequency may be specified. |
| | `--weekly=<MWF>` | Specify the days of the week on which the action should be performed. If specified, the action is repeated every seven days. Example: "MWF" executes the action every Monday, Wednesday, and Friday. Monday = M, Tuesday = TU, Wednesday = W, Thursday = TH, Friday = F, Saturday = SA, Sunday = SU. |
| | `--monthly=<DD>` | Specify the day of the month on which the action should be performed. If specified, the action is repeated every month. Multiple days may not be specified. |
| | `--yearly=<MM-DD, MM-DD,...>` | Specify the days of the year on which the action should be performed. If specified, the action is repeated every year. Dates should be specified in the format "MM-DD." Multiple dates may be comma separated. |

## SUMMARY OF  ZLMAN COMMANDS    (continued)

| command | usage/options | description |
| --- | --- | --- |
| | `--repeat=<DD:HH:MM>` | Specify the repeat frequency for the action, in the format "DD:HH:MM." Days are optional. |
| | `--gmt` | All times given are treated as GMT. If not given, all times are treated as catalog-remove-bundle (crb). Remove the association between a bundle and a catalog. |
| workstation-remove-bundle (wrb) | `zlman workstation-remove-bundle <options> <Workstation> <bundle>` | Remove the association between a device and one or more bundles. |
| workstation-list-catalogs (wlc) | `zlman workstation-list-catalogs <options> <Workstation>` | List catalogs associated with a device. |
| workstation-add-catalog (wac) | `zlman workstation-add-catalog <options> <Workstation> <catalog>` | Associate one or more catalogs with a device. |
| | `--dry-run` | |
| | `-a, --allow-removal` | |
| | `--prepare-time=<HH:MM>` | Specify a time of day at which the action should be performed. The time should be specified in the format "HH:MM," with hours in 24-hour format. |
| | `--prepare-date=<YYYY-MM-DD>` | Specify a specific date on which the action should be performed. The date should be specified in the format "YYYY-MM-DD." |
| | `--time=<HH:MM>` | Specify a time of day at which the action should be performed. The time should be specified in the format "HH:MM," with hours in 24-hour format. |

**SUMMARY OF ZLMAN COMMANDS** (continued)

| command | usage/options | description |
|---|---|---|
| | `--date=<YYYY-MM-DD>` | Specify a specific date on which the action should be performed. The date should be specified in the format "YYYY-MM-DD." |
| | `--now` | Specify that the action should be performed as soon as possible. A repeat frequency may be specified. If no other schedule is specified it defaults to now. |
| | `--relative=<DD:HH:MM>` | Specify that the action should be performed at a time relative to now. The time should be formatted as "DD:HH:MM." A repeat frequency may be specified. |
| | `--weekly=<MWF>` | Specify the days of the week on which the action should be performed. If specified, the action is repeated every seven days. Example: "MWF" executes the action every Monday, Wednesday, and Friday. Monday = M, Tuesday = TU, Wednesday = W, Thursday = TH, Friday = F, Saturday = SA, Sunday = SU. |
| | `--monthly=<DD>` | Specify the day of the month on which the action should be performed. If specified, the action is repeated every month. Multiple days may not be specified. |
| | `--yearly=<MM-DD, MM-DD,...>` | Specify the days of the year on which the action should be performed. If specified, the action is repeated every year. Dates should be specified in the format "MM-DD." Multiple dates may be comma separated. |

**SUMMARY OF ZLMAN COMMANDS** (continued)

| command | usage/options | description |
|---|---|---|
| | `--repeat=<DD:HH:MM>` | Specify the repeat frequency for the action, in the format "DD:HH:MM." Days are optional. |
| | `--gmt` | All times given are treated as GMT. If not given, all times are treated as catalog-remove-bundle (crb). Remove the association between a bundle and a catalog. |
| workstation-remove-catalog (wrc) | `zlman workstation-remove-catalog <options> <Workstation> <catalog>` | Remove the association between a device and one or more catalogs. |
| workstation-list-policies (wlp) | `zlman workstation-list-policies <options> <Workstation>` | List policies associated with a device. |
| workstation-add-policy (wap) | `zlman workstation-add-policy <options> <Workstation> <policy>` | Associate one or more policies with a device. |
| | `--time=<HH:MM>` | Specify a time of day at which the action should be performed. The time should be specified in the format "HH:MM," with hours in 24-hour format. |
| | `--date=<YYYY-MM-DD>` | Specify a specific date on which the action should be performed. The date should be specified in the format "YYYY-MM-DD." |
| | `--now` | Specify that the action should be performed as soon as possible. A repeat frequency may be specified. If no other schedule is specified it defaults to now. |

**SUMMARY OF ZLMAN COMMANDS** (continued)

| command | usage/options | description |
|---|---|---|
| | `--relative=<DD:HH:MM>` | Specify that the action should be performed at a time relative to now. The time should be formatted as "DD:HH:MM." A repeat frequency may be specified. |
| | `--weekly=<MWF>` | Specify the days of the week on which the action should be performed. If specified, the action is repeated every seven days. Example: "MWF" executes the action every Monday, Wednesday, and Friday. Monday = M, Tuesday = TU, Wednesday = W, Thursday = TH, Friday = F, Saturday = SA, Sunday = SU. |
| | `--monthly=<DD>` | Specify the day of the month on which the action should be performed. If specified, the action is repeated every month. Multiple days may not be specified. |
| | `--yearly=<MM-DD, MM-DD,...>` | Specify the days of the year on which the action should be performed. If specified, the action is repeated every year. Dates should be specified in the format "MM-DD." Multiple dates may be comma separated. |
| | `--repeat=<DD:HH:MM>` | Specify the repeat frequency for the action, in the format "DD:HH:MM." Days are optional. |
| | `--gmt` | All times given are treated as GMT. If not given, all times are treated as catalog-remove-bundle (crb). Remove the association between a bundle and a catalog. |

**SUMMARY OF ZLMAN COMMANDS** (continued)

| command | usage/options | description |
|---|---|---|
| workstation-remove-policy (wrp) | zlman workstation-remove-policy *<options>* *<Workstation>* *<policy>* | Remove the association between a device and one or more policies. |
| server-info (si) | zlman server-info *<options>* *<Server>* | Display detailed information about a device. |
| server-list (sl) | zlman server-list *<options>* *<folder>* *<filter>* | List devices in a folder. |
| | -r, --recursive | Include objects in sub-folders. |
| | -f, --filter=*<filter>* | Display only options matching the specified filter. (Wild cards * and ? may be used, if the filter is quoted.) |
| server-messages (sm) | zlman server-messages *<options>* *<Server>* | Display a list of messages associated with the specified device. |
| | -a, --all | Display all messages, including those that have been acknowledged. |
| server-ack (sa) | zlman server-ack *<options>* *<Server>* *<Log ID>* | Acknowledge a message associated with a device. |
| server-delete (sd) | zlman server-delete *<options>* *<Server>* | Delete one or more devices, folders, or groups. |
| server-refresh (sr) | zlman server-refresh *<options>* *<Server>* | Refresh the policies and bundles on one or more devices, folders, or groups. |
| | --Service=*<Service>* | Specify the name of the service to refresh on the device. If not given, all services are refreshed. |
| server-rename (srn) | zlman server-rename *<options>* *<Server>* *<New name>* | Rename a device. |
| server-move (smv) | zlman server-move *<options>* *<Server>* *<folder>* | Move a device to a different folder. |
| server-folder-create (sfc) | zlman server-folder-create *<options>* *<Name>* *<folder>* | Create a new folder. |

## SUMMARY OF ZLMAN COMMANDS   (continued)

| command | usage/options | description |
| --- | --- | --- |
| server-group-create (sgc) | zlman server-group-create <options> <Name> <folder> | Create a new group. |
| server-group-members (sgm) | zlman server-group-members <options> <Group> | List members of a group. |
| server-group-add (sga) | zlman server-group-add <options> <Group> <Server> | Add one or more devices to a group. |
| server-group-remove (sgr) | zlman server-group-remove <options> <Group> <Server> | Remove one or more members of a group. |
| server-list-bundles (slb) | zlman server-list-bundles <options> <Server> | List bundles associated with a device. |
| server-add-bundle (sab) | zlman server-add-bundle <options> <Server> <bundle> | Associate one or more bundles with a device. |
| | --dry-run | |
| | -a, --allow-removal | |
| | --prepare-time=<HH:MM> | Specify a time of day at which the action should be performed. The time should be specified in the format "HH:MM," with hours in 24-hour format. |
| | --prepare-date=<YYYY-MM-DD> | Specify a specific date on which the action should be performed. The date should be specified in the format "YYYY-MM-DD." |
| | --time=<HH:MM> | Specify a time of day at which the action should be performed. The time should be specified in the format "HH:MM," with hours in 24-hour format. |

**SUMMARY OF ZLMAN COMMANDS**   (continued)

| command | usage/options | description |
|---|---|---|
| | --date=<YYYY-MM-DD> | Specify a specific date on which the action should be performed. The date should be specified in the format "YYYY-MM-DD." |
| | --now | Specify that the action should be performed as soon as possible. A repeat frequency may be specified. If no other schedule is specified it defaults to now. |
| | --relative=<DD:HH:MM> | Specify that the action should be performed at a time relative to now. The time should be formatted as "DD:HH:MM." A repeat frequency may be specified. |
| | --weekly=<MWF> | Specify the days of the week on which the action should be performed. If specified, the action is repeated every seven days. Example: "MWF" executes the action every Monday, Wednesday, and Friday. Monday = M, Tuesday = TU, Wednesday = W, Thursday = TH, Friday = F, Saturday = SA, Sunday = SU. |
| | --monthly=<DD> | Specify the day of the month on which the action should be performed. If specified, the action is repeated every month. Multiple days may not be specified. |
| | --yearly=<MM-DD, MM-DD,...> | Specify the days of the year on which the action should be performed. If specified, the action is repeated every year. Dates should be specified in the format "MM-DD." Multiple dates may be comma separated. |

## SUMMARY OF ZLMAN COMMANDS (continued)

| command | usage/options | description |
| --- | --- | --- |
| | `--repeat=<DD:HH:MM>` | Specify the repeat frequency for the action, in the format "DD:HH:MM." Days are optional. |
| | `--gmt` | All times given are treated as GMT. If not given, all times are treated as catalog-remove-bundle (crb). Remove the association between a bundle and a catalog. |
| server-remove-bundle (srb) | `zlman server-remove-bundle <options> <Server> <bundle>` | Remove the association between a device and one or more bundles. |
| server-list-catalogs (slc) | `zlman server-list-catalogs <options> <Server>` | List catalogs associated with a device. |
| server-add-catalog (sac) | `zlman server-add-catalog <options> <Server> <catalog>` | Associate one or more catalogs with a device. |
| | `--time=<HH:MM>` | Specify a time of day at which the action should be performed. The time should be specified in the format "HH:MM," with hours in 24-hour format. |
| | `--date=<YYYY-MM-DD>` | Specify a specific date on which the action should be performed. The date should be specified in the format "YYYY-MM-DD." |
| | `--now` | Specify that the action should be performed as soon as possible. A repeat frequency may be specified. If no other schedule is specified it defaults to now. |
| | `--relative=<DD:HH:MM>` | Specify that the action should be performed at a time relative to now. The time should be formatted as "DD:HH:MM." A repeat frequency may be specified. |

**SUMMARY OF ZLMAN COMMANDS** (continued)

| command | usage/options | description |
|---|---|---|
| | `--weekly=<MWF>` | Specify the days of the week on which the action should be performed. If specified, the action is repeated every seven days. Example: "MWF" executes the action every Monday, Wednesday, and Friday. Monday = M, Tuesday = TU, Wednesday = W, Thursday = TH, Friday = F, Saturday = SA, Sunday = SU. |
| | `--monthly=<DD>` | Specify the day of the month on which the action should be performed. If specified, the action is repeated every month. Multiple days may not be specified. |
| | `--yearly=<MM-DD, MM-DD,...>` | Specify the days of the year on which the action should be performed. If specified, the action is repeated every year. Dates should be specified in the format "MM-DD." Multiple dates may be comma separated. |
| | `--repeat=<DD:HH:MM>` | Specify the repeat frequency for the action, in the format "DD:HH:MM." Days are optional. |
| | `--gmt` | All times given are treated as GMT. If not given, all times are treated as catalog-remove-bundle (crb). Remove the association between a bundle and a catalog. |
| server-remove-catalog (src) | `zlman server-remove-catalog <options> <Server> <catalog>` | Remove the association between a device and one or more catalogs. |
| server-list-policies (slp) | `zlman server-list-policies <options> <Server>` | List policies associated with a device. |

**SUMMARY OF ZLMAN COMMANDS** (continued)

| command | usage/options | description |
| --- | --- | --- |
| server-add-policy (sap) | zlman server-add-policy <options> <Server> <policy> | Associate one or more policies with a device. |
| | --time=<HH:MM> | Specify a time of day at which the action should be performed. The time should be specified in the format "HH:MM," with hours in 24-hour format. |
| | --date=<YYYY-MM-DD> | Specify a specific date on which the action should be performed. The date should be specified in the format "YYYY-MM-DD." |
| | --now | Specify that the action should be performed as soon as possible. A repeat frequency may be specified. If no other schedule is specified it defaults to now. |
| | --relative=<DD:HH:MM> | Specify that the action should be performed at a time relative to now. The time should be formatted as "DD:HH:MM." A repeat frequency may be specified. |
| | --weekly=<MWF> | Specify the days of the week on which the action should be performed. If specified, the action is repeated every seven days. Example: "MWF" executes the action every Monday, Wednesday, and Friday. Monday = M, Tuesday = TU, Wednesday = W, Thursday = TH, Friday = F, Saturday = SA, Sunday = SU. |
| | --monthly=<DD> | Specify the day of the month on which the action should be performed. If specified, the action is repeated every month. Multiple days may not be specified. |

**SUMMARY OF ZLMAN COMMANDS** (continued)

| command | usage/options | description |
| --- | --- | --- |
| | `--yearly=<MM-DD, MM-DD,...>` | Specify the days of the year on which the action should be performed. If specified, the action is repeated every year. Dates should be specified in the format "MM-DD." Multiple dates may be comma separated. |
| | `--repeat=<DD:HH:MM>` | Specify the repeat frequency for the action, in the format "DD:HH:MM." Days are optional. |
| | `--gmt` | All times given are treated as GMT. If not given, all times are treated as catalog-remove-bundle (crb). Remove the association between a bundle and a catalog. |
| `server-remove-policy (srp)` | `zlman server-remove-policy <options> <Server> <policy>` | Remove the association between a device and one or more policies. |
| `server-health (sh)` | `zlman server-health <options> <Server>` | Determine the health status of a device. |
| `ruleset-list (rsl)` | `zlman ruleset-list <options>` | List all rule sets. |
| | `-r, --recursive` | Include objects in sub-folders. |
| | `-f, --filter=<filter>` | Display only options that match the specified filter. (Wild cards * and ? may be used, if the filter is quoted.) |
| `ruleset-create-workstation (rscw)` | `zlman ruleset-create-workstation <options> <Name> <Position> <folder>` | Create a new rule set to apply when creating a workstation without a key. |
| `ruleset-create-server (rscs)` | `zlman ruleset-create-server <options> <Name> <Position> <folder>` | Create a new rule set to apply when creating a server without a key. |
| `ruleset-delete (rsd)` | `zlman ruleset-delete <options> <Name or Position>` | Remove a rule set. |

## SUMMARY OF ZLMAN COMMANDS  (continued)

| command | usage/options | description |
|---|---|---|
| ruleset-info (rsi) | zlman ruleset-info <options> <Name or Position> | Display detailed information about a ruleset. |
| ruleset-list-groups (rslg) | zlman ruleset-list-groups <options> <Name or Position> | Display a list of groups of which a device will be a member of when they are created with the specified ruleset. |
| ruleset-update (rsu) | zlman ruleset-update <options> <Name or Position> | Update a ruleset's values. |
| | -k, --newname=<key> | Specify a new name for the given ruleset. |
| | -n, --nrule=<Naming Rule> | Specify a new naming rule for the given ruleset. |
| | --workstation-folder= <Folder> | Specify a new folder in which to place workstations when they are created with the specified ruleset. |
| | --server-folder= <Folder> | Specify a new folder in which to place servers when they are created with the specified ruleset. |
| ruleset-move (rsmv) | zlman ruleset-move <options> <Name or Position> <New Position> | Change a ruleset's position. |
| ruleset-add-rule (rsar) | zlman ruleset-add-rule <options> <Name or Position> <Attribute> <Operator> <Value> | Add a rule to a ruleset. Valid attributes are Alias, AssetTag, CPU, DNS, DeviceType, GUID, HostName, IPAddress, Location, MacAddress, OS, and SubnetMask—Valid operators for strings are contains, starts, ends, equals. Valid operators for integers are <, <=, =, >, >=. |

**SUMMARY OF ZLMAN COMMANDS** (continued)

| command | usage/options | description |
| --- | --- | --- |
| ruleset-remove-rule (rsrr) | zlman ruleset-remove-rule <br> *<options> <Name or Position> <Rule Position>* | Remove a rule from a ruleset. |
| ruleset-add-workstation-group (rsaw) | zlman ruleset-add-workstation-group <br> *<options> <Name or Position> <group>* | Add a Server Group membership to objects imported with a given ruleset. |
| ruleset-add-server-group (rsas) | zlman ruleset-add-server-group *<options> <Name or Position> <group>* | Add a workstation group membership to objects imported with a given ruleset. |
| ruleset-remove-workstation-group (rsrw) | zlman ruleset-remove-workstation-group <br> *<options> <Name or Position> <group>* | Remove a workstation group membership from a ruleset. |
| ruleset-remove-server-group (rsrs) | zlman ruleset-remove-server-group *<options> <Name or Position> <group>* | Remove a server group membership from a ruleset. |
| license-info (li) | zlman license-info *<options>* | Display licensing information. |
| license-activate | zlman license-activate *<options> <key>* | Activate your system. |
| license-set-seats (lss) | zlman license-set-seats *<options> <count>* | Set the number of allowed active devices. |
| target-list (tl) | zlman target-list *<options>* | Display a list of all OS targets. |
| | -r, --recursive | Include objects in sub-folders. |
| | -f, --filter=<filter> | Display only options matching the specified filter. (Wild cards * and ? may be used, if the filter is quoted.) |
| target-create (tc) | zlman target-create *<options> <name> <arch> <Package Manager> <Primary Role> <Product Name> <Vendor> <Version> <Detect String>* | Create a new OS target. |

**SUMMARY OF ZLMAN COMMANDS**   (continued)

| command | usage/options | description |
|---|---|---|
| `target-info (ti)` | `zlman target-info` <br> `<options> <target>` | Display detailed information about an OS target. |
| `target-update` <br> `(tu)` | `zlman target-update` <br> `<options> <target>` | Modify values for a user-created OS target. |
| | `--arch=<arch>` | Specify a new arch value. |
| | `--pkgmgr=<Package Manager>` | Specify a new package manager value. |
| | `--enable` | Enable a disabled OS target. |
| | `--disable` | Disable an enabled OS target. |
| | `--role=<Primary Role>` | Specify the primary role of this target. |
| | `--product=<Product Name>` | Specify a new primary role. |
| | `--vendor=<Vendor>` | Specify a new vendor. |
| | `--detect=<Detect String>` | Specify the OS detection string. |
| | `--version=<Version>` | Specify a new version. |
| `target-delete` <br> `(td)` | `zlman target-delete` <br> `<options> <target>` | Delete a user-created OS target. |
| `queue-list (ql)` | `zlman queue-list` <br> `<options> <status>` | List all queue entries. |
| | `-r, --recursive` | Include objects in sub-folders. |
| | `-f, --filter=<filter>` | Display only options matching the specified filter. (Wild cards * and ? may be used, if the filter is quoted.) |
| `queue-reset (qr)` | `zlman queue-reset` <br> `<options> <status>` | Reset the queue. |
| `queue-flush (qf)` | `zlman queue-flush` <br> `<options> <status>` | Flush the queue. |
| `hotlist` | `zlman hotlist` <br> `<options>` | Display a list of devices that have warnings or errors. |
| `policy-list (pl)` | `zlman policy-list` <br> `<options> <folder>` <br> `<filter>` | List policies in a folder. |
| | `-r, --recursive` | Include objects in sub-folders. |

**SUMMARY OF ZLMAN COMMANDS** (continued)

| command | usage/options | description |
|---|---|---|
| | `-f, --filter=<filter>` | Display only options matching the specified filter. (Wild cards * and ? may be used, if the filter is quoted.) |
| `policy-folder-create (pfc)` | `zlman policy-folder-create <options> <name> <folder>` | Create a new folder for containing policies. |
| `policy-delete (pd)` | `zlman policy-delete <options> <policy>` | Delete a policy. |
| `policy-rename (pr)` | `zlman policy-rename <options> <name> <new name>` | Rename a policy. |
| `policy-move (pmv)` | `zlman policy-move <options> <policy> <folder>` | Move a policy. |
| `policy-group-create (pgc)` | `zlman policy-group-create <options> <Name> <folder>` | Create a policy group. |
| `policy-group-members (pgl)` | `zlman policy-group-members <options> <Group>` | List the members of a policy group. |
| `policy-group-add (pga)` | `zlman policy-group-add <options> <Group> <policy>` | Add a policy to a policy group. |
| `policy-group-remove (pgr)` | `zlman policy-group-remove <options> <Group> <policy>` | Remove a policy from a policy group. |

# rug

The following options are understood by all commands:

- `--help`—Get help on a specific command.
- `--normal-output`—Normal output (default).
- `--terse`—Terse output.
- `--quiet`—Quiet output, print only error messages.
- `--debug`—Debug output, print full exception traces.

## BUNDLE MANAGEMENT

| command | usage/options | description |
| --- | --- | --- |
| bundle-install (bin) | rug <options> bundle-install <options> | Install bundles. |
| | -y, --no-confirmation | No confirmation. |
| | -p, --prepare-only | Only prepare bundles. |
| | -f, --freshen | Freshen children. |
| | -N, --dryrun | Do a dry run. |
| bundle-list (bl) | rug <options> bundle-list | List the available bundles. |
| bundle-remove (brm) | rug <options> bundle-remove <options> | Remove bundles. |
| | -y, --no-confirmation | No confirmation. |
| | -p, --prepare-only | Only prepare bundles. |
| | -f, --freshen | Freshen children. |
| | -N, --dryrun | Do a dry run. |
| bundle-search (bse) | rug <options> bundle-search <options> | Search for bundles. |
| | -i, --installed-only | Only installed bundles. |
| bundle-upgrade (bup) | rug <options> bundle-upgrade <options> | Upgrade bundles. |
| | -y, --no-confirmation | No confirmation. |
| | -p, --prepare-only | Only prepare bundles. |
| | -f, --freshen | Freshen children. |
| | -N, --dryrun | Do a dry run. |
| catalogs (ca) | rug <options> catalogs | List the available catalogs. |
| subscribe (sub) | rug <options> subscribe <options> | Subscribe to catalogs. |

**BUNDLE MANAGEMENT**   (continued)

| command | usage/options | description |
|---|---|---|
| | `-s, --strict` | Fail if attempting to subscribe to an already-subscribed catalog. |
| | `-a, --all` | Subscribe to all catalogs. |
| unsubscribe (unsub) | `rug <options> unsubscribe <options>` | Unsubscribe to catalogs. |
| | `-s, --strict` | Fail if attempting to unsubscribe from a non-subscribed catalog. |
| | `-a, --all` | Unsubscribe from all catalogs. |

**MISCELLANEOUS**

| command | usage/options | description |
|---|---|---|
| apt-import (ai) | `rug <options> import` | Import a sources.list file from apt. |

**PACKAGE MANAGEMENT**

| command | usage/options | description |
|---|---|---|
| dump | `rug <options> dump filename` | Get an XML dump of system information. |
| file-list (fl) | `rug <options> file-list <package or file>` | List files within a package. |
| history (hi) | `rug <options> history <options> <search-string> <search-string>` | Search log entries. |
| | `-n, --search-name` | Search by package name (default). |
| | `-a, --search-action` | Search by action. |
| | `--search-host` | Search by host. |
| | `--search-user` | Search by user. |
| | `--match-all` | Require packages to match all search strings (default). |
| | `--match-any` | Allow packages to match any search string. |

## PACKAGE MANAGEMENT   (continued)

| command | usage/options | description |
|---------|---------------|-------------|
| | --match-substrings | Match search strings against any part of text. |
| | --match-words | Require search strings to match entire words. |
| | -d, --days-back | Maximum number of days to look back (default 30). |
| info (if) | rug <options> info <options> <package> <package> | Show the full info for packages. |
| | -i, --uninstalled | Search for uninstalled packages. |
| | -u, --unsubscribed | Search in unsubscribed catalogs. |
| info-conflicts (ic) | rug <options> info-conflicts <package> | List all conflicts for package. |
| info-obsoletes (io) | rug <options> info-obsoletes <package> | List all obsoletes for package. |
| info-provides (ip) | rug <options> info-provides <package> | List package's provides. |
| info-requi rements (ir) | rug <options> info-requirements <options><package> | List package's requirements. |
| | -a, --all-providers | List all packages that can satisfy a requirement. |
| | -v, --show-versions | Display full version information for packages. |
| install (in) | rug <options> install <options> | Install packages. |
| | -u, --allow-unsubscribed | Allow unsubscribed catalogs. |
| | -d, --download-only | Only download packages. |
| | --entire-catalog | Install all the packages from the catalogs specified. |
| | -N, --dry-run | Do only a dry run. |
| | -y, --no-confirmation | No confirmation. |

**PACKAGE MANAGEMENT** (continued)

| command | usage/options | description |
|---|---|---|
| list-updates (lu) | rug <options> list-updates <catalog> <catalog> | Show the available updates. |
| package-file (pf) | rug <options> package-file <file> | Get package that contains file. |
| packages (pa) | rug <options> packages <options> [catalog] [catalog] | Show the packages in a given catalog. |
| | -i, --installed-only | Show only installed packages. |
| | -u, --uninstalled-only | Show only uninstalled packages. |
| | --sort-by-name | Sort packages by name (default). |
| | --sort-by-catalog | Sort packages by catalog. |
| remove (rm) | rug <options> remove <options> | Remove packages. |
| | -N, --dry-run | Do only a dry run. |
| | -y, --no-confirmation | No confirmation. |
| search (se) | rug <options> search <options> | Search for packages matching a pattern. |
| | --match-all | Search for a match to all search strings (default). |
| | --match-any | Search for a match to any of the search strings. |
| | --match-substrings | Matches for search strings may be partial words. |
| | --match-words | Matches for search strings may be whole words. |
| | -d, --search-descriptions | Search in package descriptions, but not package names. |
| | -i, --installed-only | Show only packages that are already installed. |
| | -u, --uninstalled-only | Show only packages that are not currently installed. |

## PACKAGE MANAGEMENT   (continued)

| command | usage/options | description |
|---|---|---|
| | --locked-only | Show only locked packages. |
| | --unlocked-only | Show only unlocked packages. |
| | -c, --catalog | Show only the packages from the catalog you specify. |
| | --sort-by-name | Sort packages by name (default). |
| | --sort-by-catalog | Sort packages by catalog, not by name. |
| update (up) | rug <options> update <options> | Update packages. |
| | -d, --download-only | Only download packages. |
| | -N, --dry-run | Do only a dry run. |
| | -y, --no-confirmation | No confirmation. |
| verify (ve) | rug <options> verify <options> | Verify system dependencies. |
| | -N, --dry-run | Do only a dry run. |
| | -y, --no-confirmation | No confirmation. |
| what-conflicts (wc) | rug <options> what-conflicts <package-dep> | List packages that conflict with the item you specify. |
| what-provides (wp) | rug <options> what-provides <package-dep> | Show which packages provide a given token. |
| what-requires (wr) | rug <options> what-requires <package-dep> | Show which packages require a given token. |

## PREFERENCE MANAGEMENT

| command | usage/options | description |
|---|---|---|
| get-prefs (get) | rug <options> get-prefs <options> | List the system preferences that may be set. |
| | -d, --no-descriptions | Do not show descriptions of the preferences. |

## PREFERENCE MANAGEMENT   (continued)

| command | usage/options | description |
|---|---|---|
| set-prefs (set) | rug *<options>* set-prefs *<options>* | Set a preference variable. |
| | -s, --subscribed | List only subscribed channels. |
| | -u, --unsubscribed | List only unsubscribed channels. |
| | -m, --mounted | List only mounted channels. |
| | --show-ids | Show channel IDs. |
| | --service | List only channels in this {service}. |

## SERVICE MANAGEMENT

| command | usage/options | description |
|---|---|---|
| mount | rug *<options>* mount *<options>* *<path>* | Mount directory as a channel. |
| | -r, --recurse | Recurse into the directory. |
| | -a, --alias | Alias for new channel. |
| | -n, --name | Name for new channel. |
| refresh (ref) | rug *<options>* refresh | Refresh all or some services. |
| register (reg) | rug *<options>* register *<options>* | Register a service. |
| | -s, --service | Register against service. |
| service-add (sa) | rug *<options>* service-add *<options>* *<uri>* | Add a service. |
| | -t, --type | Type of service; default is zenworks. |
| | -d, --device-type | Type of device. |
| | -k, --key | Registration key. |
| service-delete (sd) | rug *<options>* service-delete [*<uri>* \| *<number>* \| *<name>*] | Delete a service. |

**SERVICE MANAGEMENT** (continued)

| command | usage/options | description |
| --- | --- | --- |
| service-list (sl) | rug <options><br>service-list | List the available services. |
| service-types (st) | rug <options><br>service-types | List the available service types. |

**SYSTEM**

| command | usage/options | description |
| --- | --- | --- |
| ping | rug <options><br>ping | Ping the daemon. |
| restart | rug <options><br>restart <options> | Restart the daemon. |
|  | -f, --force | Force the restart. |
| schedules (sch) | rug <options><br>schedules | Show scheduled items. |
| shutdown | rug <options><br>shutdown <options> | Shut down the daemon. |
|  | -f, --force | Force the shutdown. |

**USER MANAGEMENT**

| command | usage/options | description |
| --- | --- | --- |
| user-add (ua) | rug <options><br>user-add<br><username><br><privilege><br><privilege> | Add a new user. |
| user-delete (ud) | rug <options><br>user-delete<br><username><br><username> | Delete users. |
| user-edit (ue) | rug <options><br>user-edit | Edit an existing user. |
| user-list (ul) | rug <options><br>user-list | List users. |

# zlmmirror

The following options are understood by all commands:

-h, --help—Display a help message.

--log=[logfile]—Log messages to a specified log file.

-v, --verbose—Display verbose output.

--version—Print zlmmirror version information and exit.

## CONFIGURATION

| command | usage/options | description |
|---------|---------------|-------------|
| conf-convert (cc) | zlmmirror conf-convert <file> <new filename> | Convert the specified rcmirror.conf configuration file to the new xml format. |
| conf-generate (cg) | zlmmirror conf-generate <filename> | Create a new, empty configuration file showing all possible fields. |
| conf-validate (cv) | zlmmirror conf-<filename> validate | Check the configuration file for errors, and displays the parsed configuration information. |

## CATALOG AND BUNDLE

| command | usage/options | description |
|---------|---------------|-------------|
| bundle-list-packages (blp) | zlmmirror bundle-list-packages <options> <bundle> <catalog> | List the packages available in the specified bundle. |
| | -c,--conf=[filename] | Specify the configuration file. |
| | -t,--target | Restrict the listing to the specified target. |
| catalog-list-bundles (clb) | zlmmirror catalog-list-bundles <catalog> | List the bundles available in the specified catalog. |
| | -c,--conf=[filename] | Specify the configuration file. |
| | -t,--target | Restrict the listing to the specified target. |

**CATALOG AND BUNDLE** (continued)

| command | usage/options | description |
|---|---|---|
| catalog-list-packages (clp) | zlmmirror catalog-list-packages `<catalog>` | List the packages available in the specified catalog. |
| | -c,--conf= [`filename`] | Specify the configuration file. |
| | -t,--target | Restrict the listing to the specified target. |
| server-list-bundles (slb) | zlmmirror server-list-bundles | List the bundles available on the remote server. |
| | -p,--packages | Package set bundles in listings. |
| | -c,--conf= [filename] | Specify the configuration file. |
| | -t,--target | Restrict the listing to the specified target. |
| server-list-catalogs (slc) | zlmmirror server-list-catalogs | List the catalogs available on the remote server. |
| | -c,--conf= [filename] | Specify the configuration file. |
| | -t,--target | Restrict the listing to the specified target. |
| server-list-packages (slp) | zlmmirror server-list-packages | List the packages available on the remote server. |
| | -c,--conf= [filename] | Specify the configuration file. |
| | -t,--target | Restrict the listing to the specified target. |

**MIRROR**

| command | usage/options | description |
|---|---|---|
| mirror (m) | zlmmirror mirror | Perform the mirroring operation. |

# ZENworks Resources

Many other resources are available concerning ZENworks. This appendix describes a few to assist you in your discovery and implementation of ZENworks.

## Novell Support and Online Documentation

Novell has set up a website that is the product home for ZENworks. This website is http://www.novell.com/products/zenworks. From this website, you can find Novell's online documentation and announcements for updates to the product.

Additionally, from this page you can follow the links to http://support.novell.com/products, where you can find any patches and fixes that may be released for the product. ZENworks products are found under the NetWare and the Management Products categories.

## ZENworks Cool Solutions

Many more uses of ZENworks exist than can ever be described in a book such as this. Many customers use ZENworks every day and get very creative in their use of the system.

Novell has set up a location on the Internet where customers can go to ask their questions of the actual ZENworks engineers and see what solutions other customers have come up with for ZENworks.

The website for ZENworks Cool Solutions is http://www.novell.com/ coolsolutions/zenworks.

This site changes often and features articles from real customers or insiders on how to make ZENworks hum in your network. The site also includes a list of frequently asked questions and their answers and articles from other deployment specialists in the trenches. You can often find a white paper at the Cool Solutions site that will have the information you need for your issues.

From time to time this site also posts software that is not supported by Novell but provided by some internal Novell engineers, Novell consultants, or customers. These tools can help you in your ZENworks deployment and management.

One time on the ZENworks Cool Solutions site, the webmaster had a group of ZENworks engineers present a live, ask-the-experts session. Customers were able to ask their questions and get real-time answers for their issues. You might even see some job postings for companies looking for ZEN masters to come and implement ZENworks in their environments.

# Novell Advanced Technical Training

Novell Advanced Technical Training services provide many excellent ZENworks courses for beginners to advanced ZENworks administrators. Novell Advanced Technical Training offers their courses either online or with a Novell instructor. Whether you receive additional ZENworks training via the Internet or with a Novell instructor, you will come away knowing more about how to make ZENworks really work for you in your environment and how to get the most benefit out of the product.

Check out the website to find out more about the classes offered: http://www.novell.com/training/pep/att/def.html.

# Novell Consulting Services

Novell Consulting Services has many good engineers that are familiar with ZENworks and how it can help Novell customers in their environments. They can assist you, beyond support, in getting ZENworks to do exactly what you want for your network. Novell Consulting Services can help you with field consulting and with any custom developments you may need, tailoring ZENworks to your organization's needs.

# Novell Technical Support Services

Novell has one of the best trained and most responsive technical support service departments in the industry. Novell's technical support engineers help customers resolve installation, configuration, incompatibility, and software issues. They track those issues and create technical information documents (TIDs) that break down the symptoms and resolution to the problem. Those TIDs are available from the Novell Technical Support Knowledgebase at the following address: http://support.novell.com/search/kb_index.jsp.

You can also access the Novell Support forums to view and post messages about questions you have. Other users, as well as Novell's support engineers, can respond to these messages. The Novell Support forums are available at the following web address: http://support.novell.com/forums/.

# Index

# E

## J – K – L

## M